CW01022102

Sketchbook (3) of
Charles Rennie Mackintosh

FROM
OSCAR PATERSON
1916

2011/Tx

P+D. Dr. 10

BEGINNINGS: CHARLES RENNIE MACKINTOSH'S EARLY SKETCHES

BEGINNINGS: CHARLES RENNIE MACKINTOSH'S EARLY SKETCHES

Elaine Grogan

PUBLISHED IN ASSOCIATION WITH
THE NATIONAL LIBRARY OF IRELAND

OXFORD AMSTERDAM BOSTON LONDON NEW YORK PARIS SAN DIEGO SAN FRANCISCO SINGAPORE SYDNEY TOKYO

Architectural Press
An imprint of Elsevier Science
Linacre House, Jordan Hill, Oxford OX2 8DP
200 Wheeler Road, Burlington MA 01803

First published 2002

Copyright © 2002, National Library of Ireland. All rights reserved

The right of National Library of Ireland to be identified as the author of this work has been asserted in accordance with the Copyright, Designs and Patents Act 1988

No part of this publication may be reproduced in any material form (including photocopying or storing in any medium by electronic means and whether or not transiently or incidentally to some other use of this publication) without the written permission of the copyright holder except in accordance with the provisions of the Copyright, Designs and Patents Act 1988 or under the terms of a licence issued by the Copyright Licensing Agency Ltd, 90 Tottenham Court Road, London, England W1T 4LP. Applications for the copyright holder's written permission to reproduce any part of this publication should be addressed to the publisher

British Library Cataloguing in Publication Data
Grogan, Elaine
    Beginnings: Charles Rennie Mackintosh's early sketches
    1. Mackintosh, Charles Rennie, 1868-1928 – Notebooks, sketchbooks, etc
    2. Architecture – Sketchbooks
    I. Title 720.9'2

A catalogue record for this book is available from the British Library

Library of Congress Cataloguing in Publication Data
A catalogue record for this book is available from the Library of Congress

ISBN   0 7506 5425 2

For information on all Architectural Press publications visit our website at www.architecturalpress.com

Typeset by Microset, Witney, Oxfordshire OX28 6AL

Printed and bound in Italy by Printer Trento, S.r.l.

CONTENTS

FOREWORD: MACKINTOSH SKETCHBOOKS

From 'A close and careful study of old work', Charles Rennie Mackintosh once wrote, an artist may gather 'a great deal that will refine his tastes, that will help him to a more adequate appreciation and therefore a fuller enjoyment of art and nature and life'. To the Victorian architect, the sketchbook was an indispensable aid to both education and practice. There was – and is – nothing better than drawing to train the eye, while the forms and details that are considered worth recording can inspire new work. For some architects, the sketchbook was a compendium of useful cribs; for others, it was a spur to creation. 'Great artists don't borrow; they steal.'

Architectural sketches – or 'jottings' as Mackintosh called them – are private, a means to an end, records of ideas and motifs for future use. But they can also be drawings of beauty as well as interest. This is particularly true of Mackintosh's surviving sketchbooks. From early on he demonstrated a precision and a stylish economy of line combined with a masterly sense of composition. Even at a time when the architect's sketch and drawing had been developed to a high level of artful sophistication, his stand out as works of art and they are often enhanced by careful, mannered lettering. 'But hang it, Newbery,' exclaimed the painter James Guthrie to the director of the Glasgow School of Art on seeing some of Mackintosh's sketches from his Italian tour in an exhibition, 'the man ought to be an artist.'

The quality of Mackintosh's draughtsmanship has long been recognized and many of his sketches have been published, both for their intrinsic beauty and for what they reveal about his preoccupations and sources of inspiration. Even so, the 'discovery' of three additional sketchbooks in the National Library of Ireland is very exciting as they were made early in his career and reveal much about the buildings that interested the architect when he was still developing his ideas and personal manner of expression. One of the three, largely filled during Mackintosh's tour of Italy in 1891, is particularly interesting as it illuminates a tenuous and paradoxical connection with the other great and original Victorian Glaswegian architect of international stature, Alexander 'Greek' Thomson.

Thomson's death in 1875 – when Mackintosh was six years old – was widely lamented and a subscription was raised to set up a memorial. As one of the remarkable facts about Thomson is that he relied on his imagination and never crossed the English Channel, it seems curious that a travelling scholarship should have been established in his memory: perhaps his friends snobbishly felt that he ought really to have been abroad. No matter: the first winner of the Alexander Thomson Travelling Studentship, in 1887, was William J. Anderson. He was a good choice; he published the resulting *Architectural Studies in Italy* and later wrote a standard textbook, *The Architecture of the Renaissance in Italy*.

Three years later, at the age of 22 years, Mackintosh took the prize. The Dublin sketchbooks reveal that he made a deliberate study of Thomson's work before submitting his successful design for a public hall. The judges, however, were not unanimous and perhaps Mackintosh really ought not to have won. He certainly did not use the prize money for the 'furtherance of the study of ancient classic architecture' as the 1883 Trust deed required, and he had so little enthusiasm for antique temples that he was deterred from visiting Paestum by mere rain. Mackintosh's view of Italy was formed by John Ruskin rather than by Thomson and most buildings he sketched were Byzantine or Romanesque. Although his drawings were put to use in some of his competition entries over the next few years, he did not derive any significant benefit from his Italian tour. He was still young and inexperienced and, as his biographer Alan Crawford has concluded,

'Mackintosh had perhaps gone too soon'.

Like Thomson – but in an entirely different way – Mackintosh really did not need to travel abroad. In February 1890, shortly before he left for Italy, Mackintosh gave a lecture in Glasgow on 'Scotch Baronial Architecture' and the contents of one of the Dublin sketchbooks confirms that he was one of 'those who have harboured an early affection for the Architecture of their native land'. Later sketchbooks reveal that he was also drawn to old English architecture, while it is clear that he was very familiar with progressive 'Free Style' work south of the Border. Nevertheless, the qualities of traditional Scottish buildings – the austerity of form and idiosyncratic complexity of detail – were what always inspired him and he conveyed them in drawings that are at once precise and impressionistic.

Finally, the exquisite, exploratory sketches of flowers again reveal an attitude to nature that allied the young Scottish architect with Ruskin and the English Arts and Crafts movement; they also prefigure his preoccupations during his last years as a painter in the South of France. These Dublin sketchbooks provide a further key to understanding the powerful creative imagination of Charles Rennie Mackintosh.

Gavin Stamp
May 2002

© The Annan Gallery

ACKNOWLEDGEMENTS

I owe special thanks to Professor Michael McCarthy and Dr Christine Casey of University College, Dublin; to Deirdre Conroy and Charles Duggan, who began this study with me; to Brendan O'Donoghue and the staff of the National Library of Ireland, in particular to curators of prints and drawings, Joanna Finegan, Elizabeth M. Kirwan, Colette O'Daly and to Avice-Claire McGovern; to Dr Gavin Stamp, Dr James MacAulay and George Rawson of Glasgow School of Art and Nick Haynes of Historic Scotland for their expert advice; to Sheila Craik, Judy O'Hanlon and Oliver Grogan.

Illustrations © National Library of Ireland

INTRODUCTION

The disappearance and possible recovery of early sketches by Charles Rennie Mackintosh (1868–1928) have, from time to time, exercised scholars.[1] The decline in his reputation from 1914, when he abandoned a career in Glasgow and permanently left Scotland, resulted in the loss and destruction of much of Mackintosh's work. Undocumented early works, particularly those on paper, were inevitably the most vulnerable.

In 1991, when the name of Mackintosh was firmly re-established, three of his sketchbooks were identified in the National Library of Ireland, Dublin, by the then curator of prints and drawings, Elizabeth M. Kirwan. These works proved particularly interesting. Together, the three sketchbooks span a period of approximately ten years of the artist's early career. Some drawings may date from as early as the mid-1880s, during Mackintosh's first years as a student at the Glasgow School of Art and while he was completing his articles with the architect John Hutchison. The final sketch, showing the seed-head of the flower honesty, was made in late summer 1895 when Mackintosh was on the threshold of the most creative and successful decade of his career. As may be seen in a selection from the Dublin sketchbooks, these drawings provide a valuable record of the most significant preoccupations and experiences of the artist's formative years: his study of the architecture of Scotland's past, a tour of Italy made as a 22-year-old and, one of the central passions of Mackintosh's entire life, the study and representation of flowers.

Sketching was a facet of an all-embracing Victorian curiosity and enthusiasm for collecting. For the student-architect it was a serious work practice as well as a hobby. Intensive copying, 'a piece of pencil',[2] lay at the heart of training, both by day at an apprentice's desk and at evening classes at art school. For the professional, the sketch continued to be a central working tool. So it was with Mackintosh and his enthusiasm for his chosen career is evident in the careful observations his drawings represent. To a great extent, the early sketches show us the architect Mackintosh believed he would become, rather than the groundbreaking pioneer he actually became. Through his sketches the young man was exploring possibilities and finding his direction. At the end of the nineteenth century this still involved primarily absorbing the lessons of past masters, identifying models and paragons. However, Mackintosh's sketchbooks were more than mere portfolios of useful design ideas. Like a number of his contemporaries, he was searching for an escape from the closed circuit of revived historical styles and drawing was a means of sifting the past as he sought guiding principles on which to pin his own work.

Mackintosh's eye was uncannily observant and his pencil swift, fluid and accurate. The Dublin sketchbooks contain passages of extreme precision and, occasionally, fastidious finish. However, they were private, not made with clients in mind, nor still less for exhibition. Such studies were essentially notes, a process rather than a conclusion. Often a truncated detail was all he needed to evaluate a building, to understand its construction or to serve as a later reminder of what he had seen. Now, more than a century after these works were completed, their particular value, from the most meticulously finished to the perfunctory, is that they are Mackintosh's own record of moments in time and provide a unique glimpse of the artist at significant stages in his development.

In the period between Mackintosh's completion of the last of these drawings and their reappearance in 1991, much of his work vanished. When the sketchbooks came to light, their history, including the circumstances of their donation to the National Library of Ireland, had also been lost. On the basis of inscriptions added to each of the sketchbooks at various points in their history and by their several owners, together with circumstantial evidence, it has been possible, at least partially, to reconstruct that story. The Italian sketchbook contains the most complete of these inscriptions, apparently added at the time of donation to the library:

> Oscar Paterson was an artist in stained glass. Specimens of his work may be seen in Kirkwall Cathedral. He married Sarah Kerrigan of Birr Barracks, Eire, & I taught their eldest child – Oscar James – the violin.
> Henry Farmer of Birr.

It appears that the sketchbooks were misplaced at an early stage. Shortly after leaving Glasgow in 1914, Mackintosh himself was aware that some of his sketchbooks were no longer in his possession, specifically remembering three.[3] The Dublin botanical sketchbook seems to have been the first instance where he put Margaret Macdonald's initials on one of his works and he would have had good reason to remember – and to miss – that particular work. His Italian sketchbook would have been equally memorable. Mackintosh's loss may be explained by personal circumstances. In summer 1895, when the last of the Dublin sketchbooks was completed, he was still living with his family. Not until the end of that year or early in 1896, when the family moved to 27 Regent Park Square, did he have a room of his own. That practical consideration, together with the use of his employer's address, 140 Bath Street, on the Italian and botanical sketchbooks, suggests that Mackintosh kept such work at his office. The firm of John Honeyman and Keppie, after 1901 Honeyman, Keppie and Mackintosh, moved premises within Glasgow twice before Mackintosh left the partnership in 1913.[4] Each move would have provided the circumstances and chaos in which such small personal items could be easily overlooked or misplaced. In 1914, when the Mackintoshes packed a few suitcases and left Glasgow for what was to be an extended holiday but which became permanent exile, it would appear that the sketchbooks were not at the couple's Glasgow home.[5]

Whatever the point at which the sketchbooks became separated from Mackintosh, they were, for some period up to 1916, in the hands of the stained-glass designer, Oscar Paterson (1863–1934).[6] Each of the three sketchbooks contains a neatly cartouched inscription, *'from Oscar Paterson'*. The Italian and botanical sketchbooks have the addition, *'Bath St. Glasgow'*, the address of Paterson's studio from 1913.[7] As a fellow artist, he would have appreciated the beauty of the drawings and professional contacts, the inevitable interaction between architects and designers through shared jobs and the movement of craftspeople, no doubt

provided opportunities for him to acquire the sketchbooks. Between 1908 and 1910, Mackintosh's office and Paterson's studios were just a few doors apart, at No. 4 and No. 10 Blythswood Square. When Paterson moved to Bath Street, the centre of Glasgow's design and building world, he would again have been a close neighbour of Mackintosh, who maintained a private studio in the same street.

The date '*1916*', added to the dedicatory inscription on the Scottish sketchbook, would appear to record the occasion on which Paterson gave the sketchbooks to his friend Dr Henry George Farmer (1882–1965).[8] For the next 50 years, the most critical period for the survival of such items, as for much of Mackintosh's work, the history of the sketchbooks is bound up with the extraordinary person of Dr Farmer.

Farmer was born in Birr, Co. Offaly, Ireland, in 1882 while his father was serving as an officer with the British Army at Crinkle

Barracks. At the age of 14 years he began a career in music, playing clarinet and violin with the Royal Artillery Band in London. In 1914 he moved to Glasgow and shortly afterwards became conductor at Glasgow's foremost variety theatre, the Empire Theatre, Sauchiehall Street. A compulsively active man, Farmer was variously conductor, composer, impresario, philanthropist, writer, leading European expert on Arabic, military and Scottish music and, in his later years, music librarian at the Glasgow University Library. Although never wealthy, over his life he amassed a large and varied collection of manuscripts and memorabilia, including Mackintosh's sketchbooks. He was clearly aware of their significance. Among Farmer's books, now in basement storage at Glasgow University Library, is the catalogue of the 1933 Mackintosh Memorial Exhibition held at the McLellan Galleries, Glasgow. When the first monograph, *Charles Rennie Mackintosh and the Modern Movement* by Dr Thomas Howarth, was published in 1952 Farmer read it attentively, copying a passage into the botanical sketchbook in his possession. An enthusiastic scholar, who published books and articles on a wide range of topics, including art,[9] he may have considered cataloguing Mackintosh's drawings and it seems it was he who numbered the sketchbooks and also paginated each recto page. However, he appears not to have informed any of those involved with the recovery of Mackintosh's work that he had these drawings in his possession. He certainly never spoke of them to Howarth, who was collecting and researching the work of Mackintosh throughout the 1940s and 1950s.[10]

From the early 1950s until his death, Farmer made generous gifts to various museums and libraries: Glasgow University Library; the British Museum; Chester Beatty Library, Dublin; a district library in his native Birr; and in particular, to the National Library of Ireland. His personal papers in Glasgow

University Library show an old man absorbed with nostalgia for a remembered idyllic childhood in Ireland, a man for whom memory – remembering and being remembered – were central. It was perhaps those sentiments that prompted his particularly valuable donations to the National Library of Ireland. Among the last of his gifts, presented to the library on 27 April 1963, were the three sketchbooks of Charles Rennie Mackintosh.

Now conserved in the National Library of Ireland, these works can be seen as making an important contribution to a more intimate knowledge of the concerns and experiences of the artist in his formative years. The circumstances and the many layers of shifting meanings held by these pages for Mackintosh as he changed and grew can never be fully disentangled. Yet, Mackintosh himself provides what is perhaps an apposite summation of what his sketching meant. At the end of the surviving handwritten script for his lecture 'Seemliness' (1902) are some thoughts under the heading 'Unuttered utterances'. Among the apparently unspoken and, like his sketchbooks, private musings, Mackintosh wrote: 'Let us look upon the result of the worlds [sic] artistic achievements as the beginning[,] the morning of our lives – not the grave of our aspirations[,] the death knell of our ambitions.'[11] These early sketches provide a unique glimpse at the artist's beginnings, his point of departure and, to some degree perhaps, a clearer understanding of his genius.

Notes

1. Billcliffe, R. (1978). *Mackintosh Watercolours*. London: John Murray. Billcliffe commented on likely discoveries of both Italian and early flower drawings, p. 7.

2. Newbery, F. (1887). On the training of Architectural Students. *Royal Philosophical Society of Glasgow*, XIX, p. 190.

3. Sturrock, M. (August 1973). *Connoisseur*, Vol. 183, p. 287. Also published in Moffat, A. (1989). *Remembering Charles Rennie Mackintosh: An Illustrated Biography*, p. 79. While it is tempting to speculate that the three sketchbooks remembered by Mackintosh are those now in the National Library of Ireland, the context of the reminiscence by the daughter of Francis Newbery suggests that Mackintosh was speaking of his first three books of flower studies. These may have included the Dublin botanical sketchbook.

4. In 1906 the firm of Honeyman, Keppie and Mackintosh moved from 140 Bath Street to 4 Blythswood Square, and in 1911 to 257 West George Street. From the mid-1890s until 1914 Mackintosh maintained a private studio on Bath Street.

5. Sturrock, op. cit. note 3. Sturrock remembered that when the Mackintoshes shut up 6 Florentine Terrace in 1914, 'they left all their effects in Glasgow packing only clothes'. Later, the house was rented furnished and in 1919 was sold. William Davidson, Mackintosh's client at Windy Hill, was instrumental in saving work left at 6 Florentine Terrace (later renamed 78 Southpark Avenue) and also what remained at the Mackintoshes' Chelsea flat after the death of Margaret in 1933. This later became the basis of the Mackintosh Collection, Hunterian Art Gallery, Glasgow.

6. See Donnelly, M. (1997). *Making the Colours Sing. Scotland's Stained Glass*. Edinburgh: Stationery Office.

7. Paterson's studio was located at the following addresses: 1887–1908 at 118 West Regent Street; 1908–1912 at 10 Blythswood Square; 1913–1930 at 261 Bath Street. My thanks to Michael Donnelly for this information.

8. See *Tunic, Tinsel, Toga*, Dr Henry George Farmer centenary exhibition catalogue (1982). Glasgow University Library. Personal papers in the Farmer Collection, Glasgow University Library, contain letters indicating an easy friendship between Paterson and Farmer and the sketchbooks were almost certainly a gift between friends.

9. Cowl, C. and Craik, S. (1999). *Henry George Farmer: A Bibliography*. Glasgow University Library.

10. My thanks to Dr P. Robertson for consulting Dr Thomas Howarth on my behalf in 1999.

11. Mackintosh (1902). Seemliness. In Robertson, P, editor (1990). *The Architectural Papers*. Wendlebury: White Cockade Publishing, p. 225.

THE SCOTTISH SKETCHBOOK

Mackintosh the mature architect drew much of his inspiration from native Scottish architecture and his buildings may be seen as testimony to this debt. Howarth records that as a young man Mackintosh had toured much of Scotland.[1] The impact of those early first-hand experiences of local structures and monuments on his developing imagination was crucial. The Dublin sketchbook of Scottish architecture provides a record of his youthful sketching expeditions, in particular his visits to Crail, Culross, Stirling and Linlithgow. Together with a number of Scottish studies included in the Dublin sketchbook of Italian drawings, the Dublin sketches represent the single largest collection of Mackintosh's drawings of Scotland.

The sketchbook of Scottish architecture contains 25 pages of pencil drawings. The sequence and style of these works and Mackintosh's evolving choice of motif suggest that they belong to distinct phases in his development. The opening five pages of sketches possibly date from his early student years. These are studies of generic or standard architectural details, none of which bears an inscription: classical mouldings, Romanesque carving and Gothic roof construction as well as a page of playful variations of minaret-like spires (Figures 1 and 2). They may be seen as the work of a thorough and hard-working student at an elementary stage in his training and such motifs could as easily have been sketched from secondary sources as from life. A contemporary article, *The use and abuse of sketching and measuring*,[2] helps put such efforts in context. According to this, the purpose of student sketching was 'to train the mind and eye to what was refined and artistic, to study mouldings and details by which such effects are produced and to examine the jointing, bonding, and constructional methods by which the various parts are fitted together'.[3] The opening drawings are such studies, a student's sampler and, as if to draw an emphatic line or virtual chapter-break beneath these, Mackintosh left four ensuing pages blank.

Following this caesura, there is a marked change in both handling and subject as Mackintosh's work takes on a more serious tone of concentrated study. Pencil-lines become firmer and more confident. Hazy detailing gives way to a defter, clearer and more legible style. His interests are focused and clear themes emerge. In the remainder of the sketchbook drawings are frequently inscribed and, with one exception, were all made outside Glasgow.

Other sketchbooks contain evidence that Mackintosh used his books intermittently over extended periods[4] and for the Scottish sketchbook it may be also the case that an interval of time separates the opening drawings from those made on sketching tours. While none of the pages is dated, the year 1889 marks an important threshold in

Figure 1 – Variations, towers

Figure 2 – Gothic roof construction

Mackintosh's development and, perhaps, coincided with a change of tone in his sketching. In that year Mackintosh completed his articles and joined the firm of John Honeyman and Keppie, one of the busiest and most distinguished architectural partnerships in Glasgow. A more stimulating work environment and new colleagues would have provided mentors and fresh impulses for Mackintosh's natural enthusiasms. He had the companionship of his close friend, James Herbert McNair (1868–1955) and of the junior partner, John Keppie (1862–1945). Honeyman (1831–1914) was scholarly, with particular antiquarian and medieval interests. The firm's senior draughtsman, Alexander 'Sandy' McGibbon (1861–1938), was perhaps no less an inspiration. McGibbon also taught drawing at the Glasgow School of Art and would likely have taken a special interest in his eager and talented junior draughtsman. Such an atmosphere could well have spurred Mackintosh's self-education and explorations.

Furthermore, by the end of the 1880s the influence of Francis Newbery (1855–1946), headmaster of the Glasgow School of Art from 1885, had brought about changes in the school's philosophy and teaching practices. This new approach had the effect of encouraging students away from the mechanical copying of standard details and towards more personal and analytical drawing, particularly of vernacular buildings. In his professional capacity and at evening classes Mackintosh was drawing constantly: plans, elevations and building details. He was also creating meticulous entries for architectural competitions – with regular success, winning both the Alexander Thomson Travelling Studentship and the South Kensington National Silver Medal in 1890 and the National Gold Medal in 1892. In his private sketchbooks he was still exploring and studying, but more selectively.

Mackintosh's habit in the 1890s was to take short sketching tours and Scotland's railways provided convenient transport. The Glasgow to Edinburgh line opened in 1842 and the system developed rapidly so that, by the time of Mackintosh's sketching activities, the locations visited in the making of this sketchbook were all accessible by train. Indeed, Mackintosh's visits to Stirling and to Linlithgow were likely made in one day. Crail, the furthest point from Glasgow represented, had a train service from 1886 but it was perhaps the opening of the Forth Bridge in 1889 that facilitated Mackintosh's visits to such Fifeshire sites. For the same reason, these sites were popular with the many sketching clubs existing at that time. Like Mackintosh, these were stimulated by a new awareness of Scotland's built heritage.

Mackintosh's choice of motif was clearly not the result of accidental encounters on random wanderings. He knew what he was looking for. His interests reflect the period's reassessment of Scotland's national architecture and monuments and were a product of his own study. Lectures given by Mackintosh between 1891 and 1902 indicate that he had read widely on his chosen profession and was familiar with the standard architectural commentators of the nineteenth century: A.W.N. Pugin (1812–1852), John Ruskin (1819–1900) and Eugene-Emanuel Viollet-le-Duc (1814–1879). A book list on the final page of the Dublin sketchbook of Italian drawings, complete with references of Glasgow's Mitchell Library, shows his familiarity with current journals and publications.[5] Of particular relevance in the context of Mackintosh's Scottish drawings are works on local architectural history. *The Baronial and Ecclesiastical Antiquities of Scotland* by R.W. Billings (1813–1874), first published between 1845 and 1852, had been crucial in fostering an appreciation of Scotland's Medieval heritage and was still a standard reference in the 1890s. Mackintosh certainly knew both the text and illustrations in Billings' four volumes. At Linlithgow and Stirling the focus of Mackintosh, an heir to the Gothic Revival, was on late medieval architecture as described by Billings. Indeed, in several instances Mackintosh's drawings coincide with Billings' illustrations,[6] differing only in handling, Mackintosh's private 'jottings' being more line-bound and utilitarian.

Of particular significance to Mackintosh's developing awareness was the encyclopaedic history of Scottish architecture, *The Castellated and Domestic Architecture of Scotland* by David MacGibbon (1831–1902) and Thomas Ross (1839–1930). These books, published in five volumes between 1887 and 1892, were read closely by Mackintosh. Interestingly, all the subjects recorded in this sketchbook are singled out by MacGibbon and Ross for description in superlative terms: the oldest, the finest, etc. However, this survey of Scottish architecture was so comprehensive that it would have been impossible for Mackintosh to visit any site of historical significance that had not been mentioned. Mackintosh made extensive use of the first two volumes of MacGibbon and Ross in his 'Scotch Baronial Architecture' lecture, read to the Glasgow Architectural Association on 10 February 1891. The final drawing in the sketchbook, showing decorative details from the courtyard of Argyll's Lodgings, Stirling (Plate 13), corresponds directly to the surviving lecture text, as does one of the Scottish subjects in the Dublin sketchbook of Italian drawings, that of Amisfield Tower in Dumfries and Galloway (Plate 17). A review of the lecture in the *Architect*, 20 February 1891, refers to Mackintosh's own sketches with which he had illustrated his talk and it may well be that some of the studies in the Dublin collection were made specifically with that occasion in mind. However, whether or not these sketches had been part of Mackintosh's preparations or, indeed, were used as illustrations during delivery, the same national romanticism evident in his lecture notes can be seen in his sketching.

As a young man Mackintosh reflected many of the stresses and contradictions that characterize late Victorian architecture and in his sketching one may discern such unresolved choices of direction in the variety of approaches and treatments he adopted. These range from the atmospheric and dream-like quality of his composition *'Stirling Castle at sunset'*, displaying a romantic enchantment with the past, to the close attention paid to functional details, reflecting the practical concerns of the Arts and Crafts movement and of the current Vernacular Revival: joinery, gateposts and balustrades (Plates 5, 11 and 12). If the destinations selected by Mackintosh were signposted by his reading, he appears to have sought subjects within the distinct range of categories reflecting his dominant current interests: late medieval ecclesiastical architecture, funerary monuments, seventeenth-century decorative carving and vernacular forms.

Throughout his life Mackintosh showed a particular attraction to coastal locations, especially those frequented by artists. This was so with Crail, whose picturesque harbour and quaintly tumbledown buildings were favourites of the *plein air* painters of the 1880s and 1890s.[7] Mackintosh's interest, however, was in the tombs lining the wall in the churchyard at St Mary the Virgin and it seems likely that he travelled to Crail especially to examine its large and elaborate seventeenth-century monuments (Plate 1). The impressive scale of these was a consequence of the Scottish Church's ban, confirmed by an Act of Parliament in 1593, on burials within church buildings, a measure that had the effect of promoting ever-grander graveyard monuments. The tombs of Crail were amongst Scotland's finest, rivalled only by those at Greyfriars, Edinburgh. Mackintosh copied three adjacent monuments, the sweeps of his pencil fluently expressing the sinuous curving lines of the bulbous mouldings, hinting at weeds, weather-wear and subsidence. The architecture of death continually fascinated Mackintosh but his interest was also more than a personal one. A product of Arts and Crafts sensibilities, Mackintosh may well have viewed Crail's Anglo-Dutch sculpted stonework as prime examples of a craftsman's autonomy of invention and the richness of local traditions. His concentrated attention, with variations on a theme studied over consecutive pages, is perhaps indicative of a particularly heightened level of analysis. Interestingly, Francis Newbery, a mentor for young Mackintosh and later a life-long friend, considered such tombstones as particularly valuable headlines for students of design and he commended in particular the study of churchyards in Fife.[8]

It may also have been Newbery's influence that guided Mackintosh's eye to a similar seventeenth-century monument added to the sketchbook at Linlithgow. At the end of the nineteenth century the town was a busy industrial and commercial centre. However, it retained its medieval layout and a number of important old buildings, obvious attractions for a student of architecture.[9] The Dublin sketchbook contains five pages of Mackintosh's impressions (Plates 3, 6, 7 and 8). Curiously, these do not include the town's most famous historical building, the great ruined Palace, quoted as an influence on Mackintosh's later work, in particular the expansive masonry on the west front of the Glasgow School of Art.[10] Mackintosh was perhaps more interested in providing himself with a record of obscure views not available in commercial engravings.

Separated from the preceding drawings by a blank page is a sketch made in Glasgow Cathedral, a short distance from Mackintosh's home (Plate 4). The Cathedral was the building of architectural significance most easily accessible to him and the subject of one of his most atmospheric watercolours.[11] Nonetheless, the drawing in this sketchbook, showing the carving on the

altar of St Mary of Pity, is the only known
example of his sketching in the Cathedral's
interior. For this, he was obliged to obtain a
sketching permit from the Board of Works in
Edinburgh.[12] Honeyman, as the architect
responsible for the Cathedral's maintenance,
may well have encouraged Mackintosh to do
so.

Following the Glasgow drawing, the
sketchbook again takes up the record of
Mackintosh's explorations of rural Scotland.
He sketched vernacular subjects: an
unidentified cottage and a curious collection
of architectural details assembled on a single
page at Culross (Plate 5). Today, this small
town on the Firth of Forth has been restored
as a showpiece of sixteenth- and
seventeenth-century domestic architecture
but, at the time of Mackintosh's visit in the
early 1890s, Culross was a virtual ruin.
However, despite its abandoned and derelict
state, the town's architectural riches were
recognized, MacGibbon and Ross describing it

Figure 3 – Church of the
Holy Rude, Stirling

as 'perhaps the most striking instance of a *ville-morte* in Scotland'.[13]

From this point in the sketchbook a certain refocusing in Mackintosh's choice of subject may be discerned. His primary interest shifts from seventeenth-century funerary sculpture to medieval church architecture, in particular St Michael's Church, Linlithgow and the Church of the Holy Rude, Stirling (Plates 7, 8 and 10; Figures 3 and 4). As a young architect beginning a career in the 1890s, Mackintosh would have regarded as basic a thorough understanding of Gothic forms and an intimate knowledge of local examples. In particular, he would have regarded such studies as essential to his prospects at Honeyman and Keppie, a major part of whose practice was the restoration of old, and the design of new Gothic Revival, churches. However, if it was his employer's interests that directed Mackintosh's studies, much of his focus in this private sketchbook had a personal bias. Along with Ruskinian

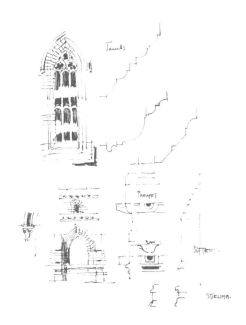

Figure 4 – Details, Church of the Holy Rude, Stirling

well-defined specifics of decoration or construction, 'bits' that might prove useful in some future project, a number of these sketches of Gothic church architecture have an open and expressive quality, seeking to capture the *gestalt* of those structures with spontaneous effect.

With its wealth of important monuments, Stirling had a strong claim on Mackintosh's attentions and, easily reached from Glasgow by train, was almost certainly visited on a number of occasions.[14] This sketchbook contains eight pages of drawings made there, including those of the Church of the Holy Rude, and provides a particularly rich concentration of Mackintosh's impressions. Among these is one of the very few examples of contemporary architecture sketched by Mackintosh. Biographers have recorded his early admiration for the architecture of James MacLaren (1843–1890) and this is confirmed in sketches of MacLaren's extension to Stirling's High School:

the observatory tower and the distinctive Zodiac door (Plate 9). MacLaren's work was completed in 1888, which gives an indication of the earliest possible date for at least this part of the sketchbook. It may even be suggested that Mackintosh's visit recorded here was homage, paid after MacLaren's death in 1890, a time when his work received particular press notice.

Strangely included in the sketchbook of Scottish architecture is a drawing that is neither Scottish nor related to the main themes explored. This drawing, perhaps the most easily overlooked in the sketchbook, is directly inside the front cover, sharing space with various inscriptions (see front endpaper). The precise pencil study shows the interweaving geometric pattern of a thirteenth-century *transenna*, now in the Museo dell'Opera del Duomo, Pisa. The brilliantly coloured mosaic was originally part of Pisa's Baptistery and at the end of the nineteenth century was displayed in the

Camposanto. This motif was copied, most likely before Mackintosh travelled to Italy, from a sketch published by William James Anderson (1863–1900), the first Alexander Thomson scholar who had toured Italy in 1888.[15] The complex geometric interplay of the cosmati work apparently fascinated Mackintosh. In Pisa, on 26 May 1891, he again sketched the mosaic fragment, this time from life. That drawing is found in the Dublin Italian sketchbook.

Plate 1

Tomb of Bailie Patrick Hunter (died 1649), St Mary the Virgin, Crail, Fifeshire

With its elaborate seventeenth-century mural tombs, the quiet churchyard of St Mary the Virgin was known as 'Westminster Abbey of Crail'. A survey of the tombs by a local historian, Erskine Beverage, published in 1893, includes a contemporary photographic record confirming Mackintosh's keen powers of observation and the accuracy of his pencil.[16] Mackintosh's admiration for Anglo-Flemish strapwork was confirmed in his 'Elizabethan architecture' lecture (1892) and forms used by seventeenth-century stone carvers were, perhaps, a source of ideas for the 'At Home' invitation card designed for the Glasgow School of Art Club (1892). Decorative work at the Glasgow Art Club (1893) also recalls the restless ribbon-like abstract patterns found on tombs at Crail.

Plate 2

The asymmetrical and almost austere cluster of buildings is typical of farms in Fifeshire. Mackintosh's attention to this anonymous house reflects his attraction to broad passages of masonry, small, irregularly placed windows and the plasticity of interlocking geometric shapes. Descriptions, at the time of its completion, of the Glasgow School of Art as 'plain', 'business-like' and 'primarily utilitarian' could equally stand for this building.[17]

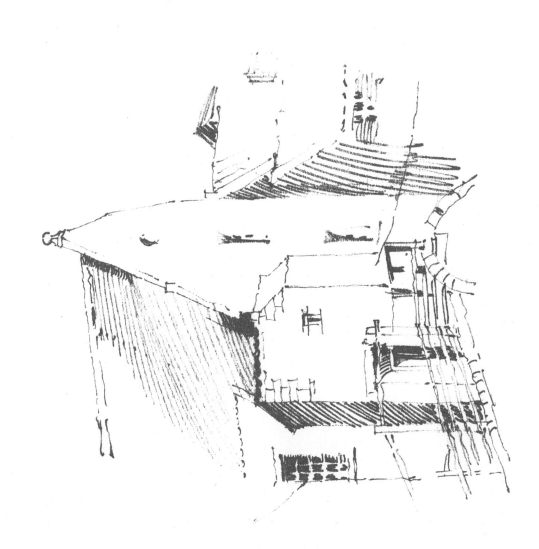

Plate 3

Kirkgate (1535), built by King James V as a grand entrance to
the Palace of Linlithgow

Inscribed: *Linlithgow   Ribs   Panel.   Jamb.*

Approached through the steep and narrow Churchwynd,
Mackintosh's worm's eye view emphasizes the dramatically
powerful mass of the fortified gateway. Deliberate hatching
representing deep shadow beneath the arched portcullis
underlines this effect. He clearly spent some time studying and
measuring the gate, including profiles of ribs and a jamb in his
sketch. Four shields carved with the orders of chivalry held by
King James V are merely indicated by impressionistic swirls.

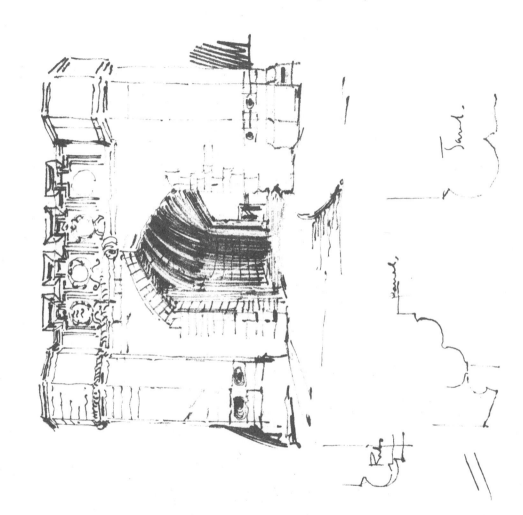

Plate 4

Side-panel, Altar of St Mary of Pity (early sixteenth century),
Glasgow Cathedral

Inscribed: *Glasgow Cath.*

The carved stone stiff-leafed capitol and episcopal stole are
symbols of the high office and building works of Archbishop
Blacader (1484–1508), who commissioned the altar forming
part of the Cathedral's prominent *Pulpitum*. John Honeyman,
the Cathedral's architect, expressed particular admiration for
the altar's *bas-relief* carving in his contribution to the
comprehensive survey, *The Book of Glasgow Cathedral*.[18]
Although this was not published until 1898, Honeyman had, no
doubt, communicated to Mackintosh his enthusiasm for an
example of fine craftsmanship. Mackintosh may also have heard
the altar's rich carving admired by Archbishop Eyre at a lecture
given to Glasgow's Archaeological Society on 21 March 1889.[19]
The clever manipulation in monochrome from *bas-relief,* the
most challenging of drawing exercises, shows Mackintosh's skill
as a draughtsman and in 1886 he had been commended at the
School of Art for such studies from casts.

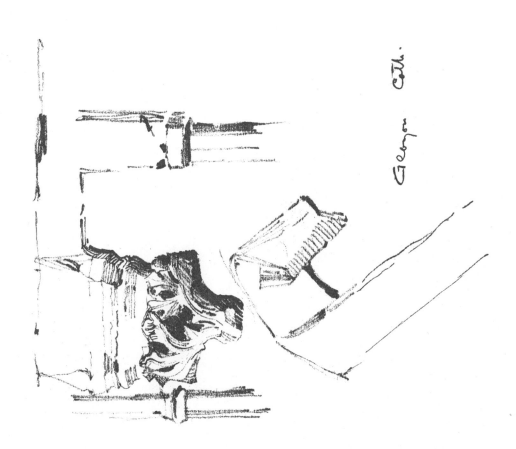

George C.M.

Plate 5

Inscribed: *Culross   Fife shire [sic]   Gate Pillar   Cornice*

The remains of sixteenth- and seventeenth-century Culross, on the Forth Estuary, provided much of interest for a historically minded young architect. Mackintosh assembled four details on a single page. The cornice profile is interesting in the context of the evolution of his aesthetic. In his own later work, he never used cornices. Indeed, during the building of the Glasgow School of Art he ordered the removal of one from above the stair, which Keppie had installed during one of Mackintosh's absences from the site.

Plate 6

Inscribed: *Linlithgow*

The loosely sketched impression of vegetation contrasts with
the more structured and precisely observed drawings in the
Dublin Botanical sketchbook. Here, the impulsive interpretation
makes identification difficult but these appear to be two species
of weeds, the lower possibly being a sow-thistle. Mackintosh's
attention recalls Ruskin's observations: 'There is not a cluster of
weeds growing in any cranny of a ruin which has not a beauty
in all respects nearly equal, and in some, immeasurably superior,
to that of the most elaborate sculpture of its stone.'[20]

Plate 7

Apse, St Michael's, Linlithgow (thirteenth to sixteenth century)

Inscribed: *Linlithgow*

The three-sided apse was added to enlarge St Michael's in
1531. Consequent tell-tale irregularities in the details of the
apse and along the nave parapet are most obvious from the
southeast corner of the churchyard, from where Mackintosh
sketched. Buttress niches, empty of their statues since the
iconoclasm of the Reformation, are clearly pencilled. At Queen's
Cross Church (1897) Mackintosh used the conceit of the
empty niche in a faint, yet curious, echo of what he had
sketched here. Between 1894 and 1897 the firm of Honeyman
and Keppie carried out major restoration work at St Michael's
and Mackintosh may have been involved in that project.

Plate 8

South elevation, St Michael's, Linlithgow

Inscribed: *Jamb.   Base   Sill.   Linlithgow*

Mackintosh may have recalled Billings' observations as he
sketched: 'The church, dedicated to St. Michael, deserves some
attention, because it is assuredly the most important specimen
of an ancient parochial church now existing in Scotland both as
to dimensions and real architectural interest. The architecture is
richly and variedly decorated and no two windows on the
same side are of similar design, a characteristic distinctly
noticeable in the view from the south.'[21] Mackintosh's sketch of
two bays of the south aisle and clerestory shows that variety in
windows. Beneath and to the left of his sketch are detailed
studies of windowsill and jamb profiles and the projecting base
of a buttress.

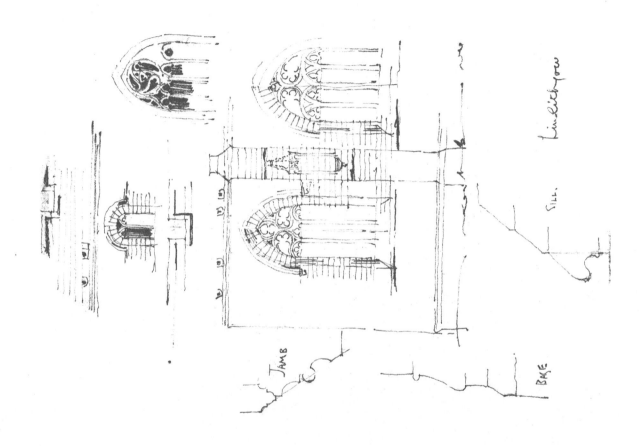

JAMB

BASE

SILL.

Linlithgow

Plate 9

Right and below: observatory tower and Zodiac door of
Stirling High School Extension (1888) by James MacLaren
(1843–1890)
Left: tower added to Stirling's fifteenth-century Tolbooth in
1705 by Sir William Bruce (1630–1710)

Inscribed: *Stirling*

Similarities between MacLaren's observatory tower and the
water-tower designed by Mackintosh for the Glasgow Herald
Building (1893) have been noted.[22] Strangely juxtaposed with
the work of MacLaren, an admired near-contemporary, is Sir
William Bruce's tower at Stirling's Tolbooth. Mackintosh could
have been expected to have little sympathy for the work of
Bruce, Scotland's main interpreter of Wrenian classical
architecture. In his 'Scotch Baronial Architecture' lecture he
deplored the dilution of indigenous styles by imported forms
and may well have had the Francophile Bruce in mind in that
respect. Nonetheless, he was obviously interested in studying
this structure, picking out the lace-like wrought-iron work,
which edges the curves of the tower's ogee spire, in a series of
emphatic dots.

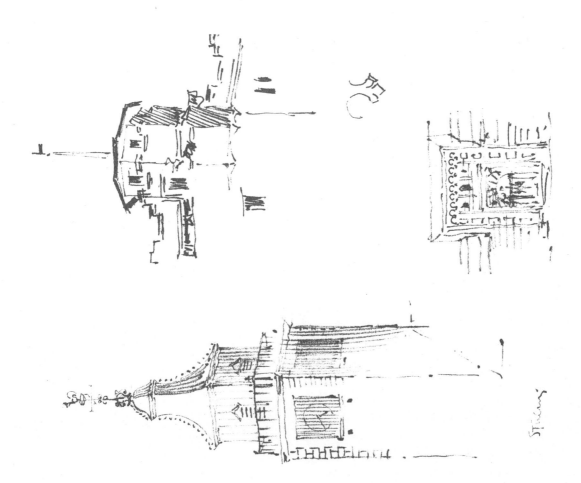

Plate 10

West Tower, Church of the Holy Rude, Stirling

Inscribed: *Corbeling [sic]   Jambs.   Stirling.*

Sketched from the northwest corner of the churchyard, this
study provided Mackintosh with examples of two periods in
Scottish architectural history as outlined by MacGibbon and
Ross and interpreted by Mackintosh in his 'Scotch Baronial
Architecture' lecture. The strong masonry massing and the
defensive features of the tower's lower section belong to the
fifteenth century. In the upper storey, a later extension, an
elegance characteristic of a different age is evident. Battlements
become decorative conceits and the treatment of window
ornamentation is more sophisticated and stately, hinting at
Renaissance sensibilities.

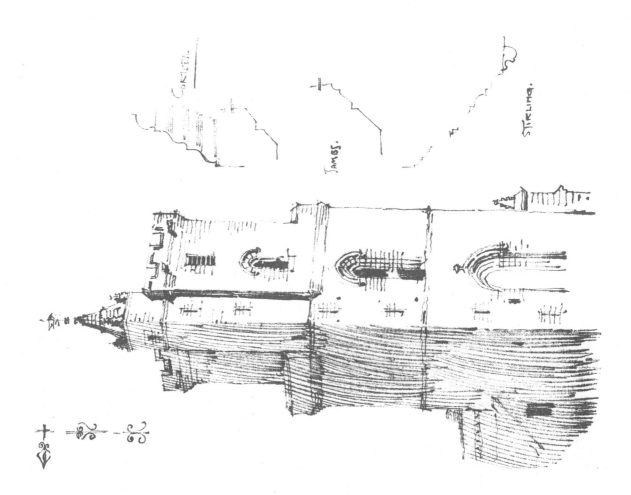

Plate 11

Balustrade, Cowane's Hospital (1649), Stirling

With a Japanese simplicity of line and using no shading or
hatching, the balustrade at Cowane's Hospital is shown as a
floating shape, isolated from its surroundings.

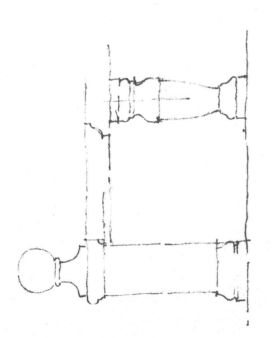

Plate 12

Signed and inscribed: *Stirling Castle at sunset.   C.R.M.*

Mackintosh responded to Stirling Castle, dramatically silhouetted against the evening sky, as an artist rather than as an architect and, significantly, this is the only signed drawing in the sketchbook. Billings' description might be recalled: 'It is difficult to say which is calculated to give greater pleasure to the sightseer – the view of Stirling Castle itself, from the plain below and the surrounding hills, or the panoramic prospect from the battlements, of which the edifice itself forms no part. Both possess in high perfection all the attributions which travellers seek in such scenes. The buildings rise from a perpendicular rock; they are ancient, varied in outline and not only picturesque but highly ornamental.'[23] Mackintosh's enduring obsession with man-made structures built on rocky outcrops is evident in one of his last paintings, *Le Fort Maillert* (1927).

STIRLING CASTLE
AT SUNSET. C.R.M.

Plate 13

Inscribed: *Argyls [sic] Lodging Stirling.*

In the early 1890s Argyll's Lodgings was a military hospital, a use welcomed by MacGibbon and Ross as helping to preserve the fabric of the seventeenth-century town mansion. Mackintosh sketched six examples of the ornamental strapwork on the pediments in the *Cour d'Honneur*, including that of the main door. His choice of motif relates directly to the text of the 'Scotch Baronial Architecture' lecture: 'This is probably the finest specimen of an old town residence remaining in Scotland. The building forms three sides of a square round an irregular courtyard. There are some fine examples here of the enriched pediments of interlacing ornament so frequently seen in 17th Centy work.'[24]

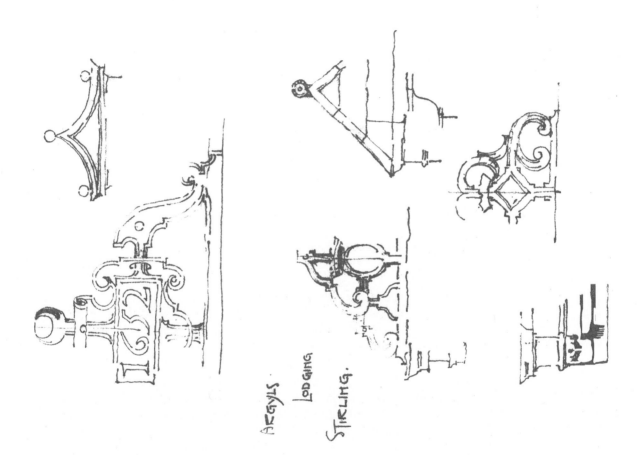

ARGYLS
LODGING
STIRLING.

Notes

1. Howarth, T. (1952, 2nd edn 1977). *Charles Rennie Mackintosh and the Modern Movement*. London: Routledge & Kegan Paul, p. 2.

2. Cresswell, H.O. (11 April 1891). The use and abuse of sketching and measuring. *Builder*, 60, pp. 292–296.

3. Cresswell, ibid., p. 292.

4. The Dublin sketchbooks of Italian drawings and of flower drawings both contain evidence that they were used over several years.

5. See Appendix I.

6. Billings, R.W. (1845–1852). *The Baronial and Ecclesiastical Antiquities of Scotland*. Edinburgh: Edmonston and Douglas. 'Outer Gateway of the Palace, Linlithgow' (Ill.) Vol. III, plate 57. 'The South View, Church of St. Michael's, Linlithgow' (Ill.) Vol. III, plate 53. MacGibbon and Ross also illustrated the kirkgate at Linlithgow, Vol. I, figure 429.

7. For example, William York MacGregor (RSA, 1855–1923), *Crail* (oil, 1883). Smith Art Gallery and Museum, Stirling.

8. Newbery, F. (1893). Art in relation to technical education. *Evening Times*, 12 April. Newbery's article was based on his lectures and Mackintosh had almost certainly heard his recommendations. My thanks to G. Rawson for pointing out this article.

9. Mackintosh's entry for the 1892 Pugin Travelling Studentship included sketches of Linlithgow. See *Building News* (22 January 1892) and *Builder* (30 January 1892), 62, p. 81.

10. Grigor, M. and Murphy, R. (1993). *The Architect's Architect*. London: Bellew, p. 25.

11. Mackintosh, *Glasgow Cathedral at Sunset* (1890). Glasgow University collection.

12. Edwards, B. (1984). John Honeyman, Victorian Architect and Restorer and Partner of Charles Rennie Mackintosh. *CRM Society Newsletter*, 36, p. 8. Quoting Honeyman's presidential address to the Glasgow Archaeological Society, 1888.

13. MacGibbon D. and Ross, T. (1892). *The Castellated and Domestic Architecture of Scotland*. Edinburgh: David Douglas, Vol. V, p. 26.

14. Howarth's chronology lists Stirling among sites visited in 1894. The 1933 Mackintosh Memorial Exhibition included a watercolour of Stirling's old High Church (1894), untraced.

15. Anderson, W.J. (1890). *Architectural Studies in Italy*. Glasgow: Maclure, MacDonald & Co., plate IV. William James Anderson (1863–1900) won the Thomson Studentship in 1887 and travelled to Italy the following year. In 1894 he joined the staff at Glasgow School of Art and in 1896 became director of the architecture department.

16. Beverage, Erskine (1893). *The Churchyard Memorials of Crail*. Edinburgh: T. & A. Constable.

17. Prominent profiles (11 December 1909). *Evening Times*, Glasgow.

18. Eyre-Todd, G., editor (1898). *The Book of Glasgow Cathedral, A History and Description*. Glasgow: Morison Brothers, p. 266.

19. Ibid., p. 308. The lecture, 'The odd arrangements of Glasgow Cathedral', by Archbishop Eyre, formed the basis of a chapter 'The ancient altars of the Cathedral', in *The Book of Glasgow Cathedral*. The south panel of the Altar, that sketched by Mackintosh, received particular comment.

20. Ruskin, J. (1886). *Seven Lamps of Architecture* (5th edition). London: George Allen (Truth, xix), p. 53.

21. Billings, op. cit., note 6. Vol. III, Linlithgow, p. 3.

22. Walker, D. (November 1968). Charles Rennie Mackintosh. *The Architectural Review*, p. 363.

23. Billings, op. cit., note 6. Vol. IV, Stirling, p. 1.

24. Mackintosh (1891). Scotch Baronial Architecture. In Robertson, P, editor (1990). *The Architectural Papers*, p. 61.

THE ITALIAN SKETCHBOOK

When the 22-year-old Mackintosh, on the strength of the Alexander Thomson Travelling Studentship, set out for Italy in spring 1891, he had among the drawing material in his luggage a small pocket sketchbook. He arrived in Naples on Sunday 5 April and over the following eight weeks, for approximately two-thirds of his tour, this sketchbook was in constant use. Indeed, the conditions of his Studentship stipulated that such records were to be presented to the trustees on the recipient's return. Thus, unlike the other two sketchbooks in Dublin, the Italian sketchbook was not solely private.

Extraordinarily, the sketchbook that the budding young professional took with him to Italy was already almost half full. Up to 41 of the opening drawings had been made in Scotland. From evidence dating those drawings it would appear that the sketchbook had been in intermittent use for at least three years before the Italian visit and Mackintosh may also have added to it after returning from Italy (Plate 20). When he opened this sketchbook to sketch for the first time in Italy, before the Chiesa del Carmine in Naples, he turned to the middle. Throughout April and May it was constantly in use and, when he reached Venice in the early days of June, nearly every page was filled. At this stage the sketchbook was a densely packed and complex weave, crammed with pencil studies: clear perspective drawings, closely observed details, picturesque 'Sunday' sketches and thumbnail impressions. Mackintosh's hand varies from a bold linear clarity to a fidgety, twitching nervousness and, in several cases, an almost painterly handling of nuance and pencil-tones. The result is a curious mixing of time and place, styles and motifs, which present a challenge to a 'reader'. Yet, perhaps, this sketchbook is all the more revealing of the young artist, his immature uncertainties as well as his firmly held beliefs.

The opening sketches made before

Figure 5 – Details, 1888 International Exhibition Hall, Glasgow

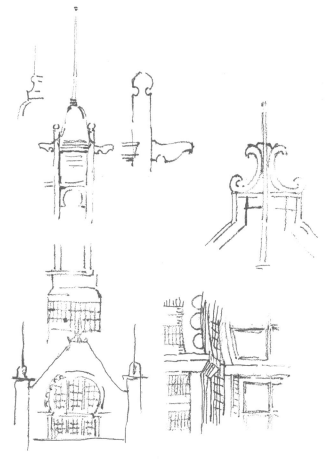

Mackintosh left for Italy are an intriguingly varied assembly.

Mackintosh's early admiration for James Sellars (1843–1888) is reflected in drawings of Sellars' Exhibition Hall for the Glasgow International Exhibition in 1888 (Plate 15 and Figure 5). This was a temporary structure, demolished shortly after the exhibition closed in November of that year. Mackintosh almost certainly had visited this, the most talked-about building in Glasgow at that time. He would also have been conscious that the head of the Glasgow School of Art, Francis Newbery, was one of the exhibition's convenors. Apparently fascinated by the sheer exotic exuberance of Sellars' eastern confection, Macintosh sketched at least four pages of details. Although illustrated in contemporary journals and recorded in photographs, his 'notes' appear to have been sketched directly from the building before its demolition.

Also among the opening drawings are several pages of 'bits', brief illustrations of doorframes and windows, the sort of reference notes a young architect in the eclectic late Victorian milieu might expect to use with handsome effect in the course of a career. Other motifs were copied from published sources (Plate 16). Mackintosh was, no doubt, in constant search of ideas, scanning material with a ready pencil, and at least two pages in this sketchbook were taken from illustrations in the *Architect*, issues more than 10-years-old when Mackintosh used them.[1] McNair recalled that during quiet days at the office both he and Mackintosh sketched and doodled. One may imagine that it was on such occasions that these leisurely pencil dreams were made.

The date '7 May 1890', inscribed on several pages, places these works at an interesting point in Mackintosh's career (Plate 21). In September 1890 he was awarded the Thomson Studentship. In the spring of that year he had almost certainly been preoccupied with his competition entry, a public hall designed in a suitably classical style. His sketch of Alexander Thomson's Cairney Building would seem to have been an ambitious young man's research as he prepared his competition project (Plate 22). Other pages containing neo-Greek and Thomsonesque features were perhaps also part of his thinking as he designed his winning entry (Figure 6). Examples of such generic repeat-ornamentation were readily available on Glasgow's fashionable terraces, including those designed by Thomson. Mackintosh would have consulted reference books also, in particular Owen Jones's *The Grammar of Ornament*. A book list on the final page of this sketchbook lists such a pattern-book, *Architectural Ornament of All Nations*, which contains plates of similar Greek ornament.[2]

The three months that Mackintosh spent in Italy are the most comprehensively documented period of his career. He kept a

Figure 6 – Thomsonesque ornament

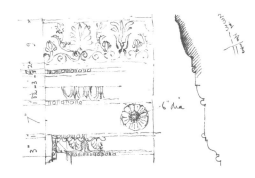

diary, a condition of his Studentship, and in addition he lectured on his experiences in the following year.[3] Surviving drawings, including the Dublin sketchbook, constitute a valuable visual record of his journey and compensate for his sometimes incomplete written notes.

Before departing for Italy, Mackintosh had planned his journey and, no doubt, those preparations primed his attentions and guided his choice of motif. Howarth records that Mackintosh had read Ruskin and Baedeker.[4] As well as reading, Mackintosh would have consulted others about his coming tour. It is known that he met William James Anderson (1863–1900), the winner of the 1887 Thomson Studentship,[5] when Anderson chaired Mackintosh's 'Scotch Baronial Architecture' lecture. His copy of a sketch by Anderson, seen in the Scottish sketchbook, is evidence of Mackintosh's interest in his predecessor's Italian experiences and, to some extent, Anderson's admiration for certain Renaissance buildings may have influenced Mackintosh's sketching.

With the development of photomechanical reproduction, views of Italian architecture, landscapes and city scenes became widely available and from those Mackintosh would have been already familiar with the principal historic buildings of Italy. In Florence, his diary records buying photographs. He may well have done so in other Italian cities also and this may explain why he did not draw the most famous buildings, for instance the *Duomo* in Florence or the famous campanile at Pisa. Nonetheless, like Grand Tourists since the eighteenth century, Mackintosh's itinerary focused on the principal centres of artistic and architectural significance and the motifs he selected were usually to be found within a narrow radius of the historic centre and close to the railway station of the towns he visited. With few exceptions, he limited himself to landmark buildings, an inner circle of canonical architecture admired by Ruskin, listed in Baedeker and pointed out by others. While this was the understandable approach of an ambitious young tourist restricted by time, money and transport, and keen not to miss key structures amidst the riches of Italy, the conservative range of his subjects is striking and contrasts with his later revolutionary vision. Travelling by train, he visited over 25 cities in three months. Ruskin had warned of the detrimental effects of swifter rail transport, deploring the rush from one city to the next, with the tourist experiencing a confusing whirl of palaces and churches.[6] For Mackintosh, sketching must have provided an important filter for such a crowding of impressions and an anchor for his memory.

The eagerness of Mackintosh's first diary entries suggests that he arrived in Naples with the intention of learning as much as possible from his experiences. However, this eagerness may have become the victim of what the contemporary travel writer, Augustus Hare referred to as 'the problems of the south': miserable inns, insects and disgusting food.[7] In his first two weeks in Italy this sketchbook was used just twice (Plates 25 and 26). Only the briefest 'notes' were added at Orvieto and none during his nine-day stay in Siena (Figure 7). Nonetheless, it must be remembered that this sketchbook was not the only drawing material in use. A number of loose sketches and delicate watercolours from the same period have survived; there may well have been others that have not.

Figure 7 – Details, Orvieto

52

From southern Italy Mackintosh travelled northwards to Rome. He marked the change in location by leaving two pages of his sketchbook blank and during his 16-day stay there he used just five pages (Plates 28 and 29). His sketching activity in Rome bears out a somewhat cavalier approach to the area of study specified by the terms of his Studentship: 'the study of Ancient Classical Architecture as practised prior to the commencement of the third century of the Christian era'.[8] Rome, more than anywhere else, would have furnished Mackintosh with the opportunity to meet those terms. In the entire sketchbook few drawings fulfil the conditions of his bursary and, in Rome, no single sketch meets them. Loyal to prejudices absorbed with his reading of Ruskin, Mackintosh appears to have been entirely unmoved by classical forms and his reaction to parts of ancient Rome was one of abhorrence, later referring to the Forum and Capitol as 'delapidated & decrepit [sic].'[9]

Mackintosh was a young man alone abroad for the first time and a significant entry in his diary is that of 10 May, in Siena: 'Went down to dinner and found Paxton and a fellow Dods sitting there. It turned out rather lucky for me as I found out.' James Paxton and Robert Smith Dods became Mackintosh's travelling companions until the second week of June.[10] Thus, for most of the period this sketchbook was in use, Mackintosh was not travelling alone. Indeed, the gathering pace of his work suggests that having company may somehow have released his energies.

At the time Mackintosh was travelling mass tourism was already a fact in Italy and Florence was the focal point, as Rome had been for the more leisurely visitor of the eighteenth century. Ruskin found the city 'a most tormenting and harassing place' and commented: 'In Florence one feels always in a shop.'[11] Henry James also conjures an image of a city thronged with tourists and street traders.[12] During his week in Florence Mackintosh apparently realized the extravagance of leaving pages of his sketchbook unused. Money was a constant concern, as evidenced by his correspondence with the secretary of the Thomson Memorial Trust.[13] Quality drawing paper was expensive and perhaps finding supplies in a strange city and making the purchase in a foreign language daunted the young man. In Florence, when he had already been in Italy for over six weeks, he turned back over drawings made since his arrival to pages left empty when he began sketching in Naples. From this point his sketching weaves backwards and forwards as he returned to pages previously left blank, skipped pages, only to return again. He also began to fill spaces on pages already used. In the crowded and narrow streets of Florence his use of the sketchbook began to take on an intensity as pages were crammed and it became the overflowing cornucopia of images it now is. Often a page was added to over several days and without regard for unity of scale. While Mackintosh's juxtaposition of work within his sketchbook may have had some personal internal logic, the result is that the drawings do not present themselves neatly, following the chronology of his journey.

One page in particular reveals something of Mackintosh's sketching habits. In Florence he sketched the dome and the campanile of the sacristy at S. Spirito (Plate 30). Completing a neat pyramidal composition is a chimney cluster. His choice is an interesting mix of an Arts and Crafts attention to mundane or functional elements and of grander aspirations, here perhaps reflecting Anderson's influence.[14] He continued to sketch in Florence, filling the ensuing eight pages. Later, most likely on 26 May while en route from Florence to Pisa, he returned to this page and in the left-hand corner he sketched the upper part of the bell tower of S. Stefano degli Agostiniani in Empoli. This small Tuscan town is not mentioned either in

Mackintosh's diary nor in his Italian lecture and this tiny thumbnail sketch is now the only suggestion that he might ever have visited it.

In the week spent travelling from Florence to Venice, Mackintosh made frequent use of the sketchbook. He spent a day each at Pisa and Pistoia (Plates 37–41; Figure 8). No doubt influenced by Ruskin's dislike of Bologna, he stayed just two hours. Perhaps leaving his luggage at the *Deposito*, he found time to eat and to sketch the campanile of the Cattedrale di S. Pietro, mistakenly inscribing it as the '*Duomo*' (Plate 42). Later, in Ravenna, he returned to this page and, in a particularly distinctive and seemingly conscious juxtaposition, he placed the tower of S. Giovanni Evangelista, alongside that of S. Pietro. He continued to leave occasional pages blank, for example between Bologna and Ravenna. That page was subsequently used in Ferrara (Plate 43). When he reached Venice, where he celebrated his 23rd birthday, he had come to the end of this sketchbook. In Verona he began a fresh sketchbook, now in the Glasgow School of Art, and in this he recorded the final four weeks of his tour.

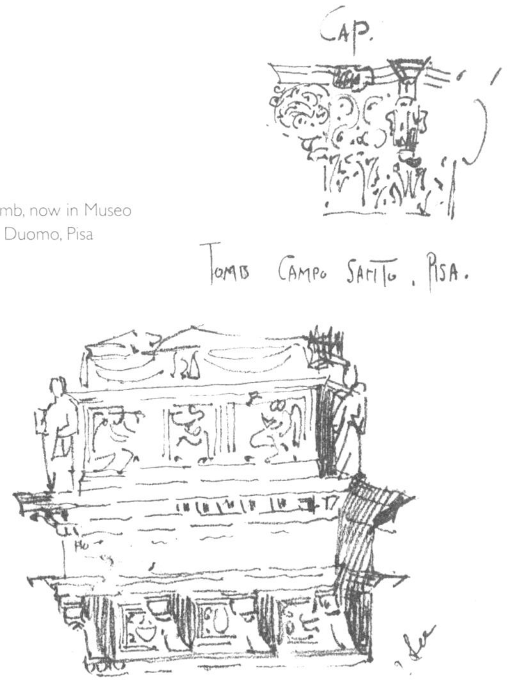

Figure 8 – Tomb, now in Museo dell'Opera del Duomo, Pisa

Mackintosh's sketching suggests that he had little interest in the contemporary buildings of the new Italy. Neither was he travelling with the eyes of an historian. That is clear from the treatment and descriptions in his later 'A Tour in Italy' lecture, when he emphasized the value of spontaneous 'impressions', avoiding 'dry & tiresome' data.[15] Nonetheless, in many respects the motifs he selected for this sketchbook appear to be programmatic. In more than 47 pages of Italian drawings certain specific themes were favoured. In particular, the recurrence of Renaissance *palazzi* is striking, an admiration confirmed in his lecture: 'The beautiful simplicity, the large masses of plain masonry & small windows, surmounted by tremendeous [sic] cornices beautifully designed, gives these palaces a simple but dignified grandeur.'[16] He sketched those admired by Ruskin: the Palazzo Vecchio in Florence and Palazzo Agostini in Pisa. The link between a series of severely elegant Florentine mansions featured in the sketchbook is, perhaps, their design by architects in the circle of Giuliano da Sangallo (1445–1516), a selection that may reflect the recommendations of Anderson (Plates 29–31, 33–35). One might also wonder whether Mackintosh had seen the sketchbooks of Sangallo on one of his three visits to the Vatican Museum.[17] Those drawings would likely have appealed to Mackintosh, who, like Sangallo, was in pursuit of something fresh from the study of the old.

Other themes reflect a more personal aesthetic already formed in Scotland. Most obviously, Mackintosh's preferred Scottish themes may be seen in tombs he sketched in Pisa's Camposanto and now in the Museo dell'Opera del Duomo (Figure 8). His study of the brick structures of Italy reflects his particular interest in masonry and in the techniques of his profession. Also, his fascination with the distinctive vertical lines of the Italian campanile, of which there are 15 examples, can be seen in the same light as his

affection for Scottish towers sketched in this book before departing for Italy (Plates 17, 18 and 23; Figure 9). Like the architect George

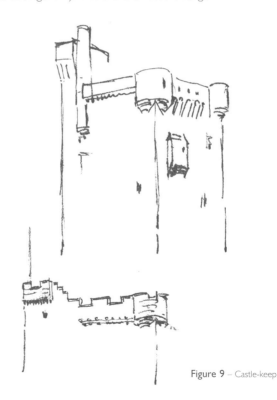

Figure 9 – Castle-keep

Edmund Street,[18] Mackintosh was apparently struck by the seemingly endless range of subtle variations in the structure of the campanile. His later use of verticals, from his early work at the Glasgow Herald Building (1893) to one of his last executed buildings, the west front of the Glasgow School of Art (1906–1909), may be seen as recalling his response to the form of the Italian campanile.

As part of a generation eager to break free of historicism, Mackintosh subscribed to Pugin's cleansing precept of decorating construction rather than constructing decoration and an important recurring theme in this sketchbook is the study of the decorative treatment of functional elements. His several observations of ironwork anticipate the attention he gave to wrought-iron in his own later designs (Figure 10). Doors, together with chimneys, are among the few anonymous, non-canonical features appearing in the sketchbook. Doors, in particular, form a distinctive *leitmotif*. In his

mature works, entrances frequently became concentrated points for his creative imagination and it may be suggested that ornamented doorways sketched in Italy left some resonance in his memory. The monumental doorway of the Palazzo Schifanoia, Ferrara, may well have informed his

Figure 10 – Details, Ravenna

treatment of doors and windows in the 1892 Glasgow Art Gallery competition design (Plate 43). In later work the memory is less direct, and possibly subliminal. The main entrance of the Glasgow School of Art is a careful balance of plainness and monumentality. Like the portals sketched at Ravenna, the School's entrance has a central post with the decoration gathered in a *sopraporta* (Plates 39 and 41).

Mackintosh's diary records a number of museum visits and at least ten pages of this sketchbook were completed in museums. In Florence, he sketched in the Museo Nazionale del Bargello. He visited the Uffizi, where he ran 'like a butterfly in a garden',[19] and, on the same day, the Palazzo Pitti (Plate 27). At Ravenna he visited the Museo Arcivescovile and a museum in the Classe Monastery (Plates 39, 41 and 44). It has been commented that Mackintosh went to Italy too soon.[20] Certainly, if this journey had been made at a later point in his development, he might well have heeded the precept of the Arts and Crafts designer, J.D. Sedding: 'No more museum art.'[21] As 'a small lad',[22] his later words to describe the younger self who toured Italy, Mackintosh was still a product of his training, copying the best of the past, and museums offered a convenient guarantee of quality and significance.

Much of the sketchbook is an ambitious young man's study of correct models, of what it might take to be successful and, seemingly, this is how it was used on Mackintosh's return to Scotland. First-hand knowledge of the masterworks of the great Italian architects gave him both confidence and ideas as he established himself as a young man of promise in architectural circles in Glasgow. The dome of S. Spirito may be seen in his Chapter House design (1892 Soane Medallion competition). Lessons absorbed while sketching the square towers of S. Pietro, Bologna and S. Giovanni Evangelista, Ravenna, may have been useful as he worked on the

Glasgow Art Gallery competition entry (1892).

However, the effects of Mackintosh's Italian experiences cannot be measured and accounted for in so many echoes of motifs and re-workings of models. As with his Scottish drawings, these pages represent only part of his experiences. Perhaps the most important and enduring after-effect of his intense observations is not so much in the concrete as in essence. As his tour progressed, the drawing becomes noticeably more relaxed. Earnest architectural 'notes' are increasingly replaced by impressions and vignettes: countrywomen walking to church or market, the prow of a gondola. Occasionally the sketches also hint at the dynamics of sunlight, in sudden sharply defined shapes and in the quick, close hatching of deep shadows in narrow streets. The clarity of southern light, which throws every building into stark contrasts of void and mass, light and shade, was perhaps a critical spark in the development of Mackintosh's particular architectural vision. Even after direct models were rejected and forgotten, the underlying experiences and sensations may have remained as an indefinable ingredient in his memory. To that extent, these drawings may be seen as a vital preliminary stage in his formation.

Plate 14

Inscribed: *A Country Church*

Judges of the 1892 Pugin Studentship, a competition Mackintosh
entered unsuccessfully, warned against 'pretty sketches', as
having little practical value for a student of architecture.[23] In his
private sketchbooks Mackintosh did not limit his study to
prescribed or purposeful collations of useful motifs. Here, the
picturesque charm and atmosphere of a country church
becomes the subject. The church's lych gate is similarly sketched
for the motif's romantic appeal rather than merely as a closely
observed record of its architecture.

A COUNTRY CHURCH

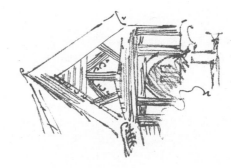

Plate 15

Glasgow's International Exhibition Hall, 1888, by Campbell Douglas and James Sellars, assisted by John Keppie

The buildings for Glasgow's 1888 International Exhibition demonstrated a late Victorian relish for oriental and exotic effects. Designed as purely temporary structures, and largely constructed of wood, they featured unusual decorative elements. The overall impression has been described as 'a mishmash of Byzantine, Moorish and Indian influences, dubbed "Baghdad by Kelvinside"'.[24] The 20-year-old Mackintosh was clearly fascinated and he sketched several pages of details as well as this view of one of the towers belonging to the Main Exhibition Hall.

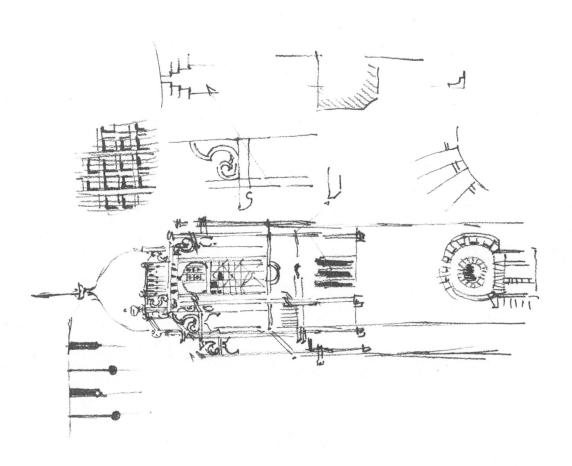

Plate 16

Window and details, Kilnaughten Church, County Limerick, Ireland

Inscribed: *An Irish Sketch.*

Motifs on this page were copied from the *Architect*, 'Examples of late Irish Architecture drawn by J. L. Robinson', Vol. 18, 15 December 1877. The accompanying text interestingly reflects what Mackintosh had to say of native Scottish architectural history in his 'Scotch Baronial Architecture' lecture: 'Although the architectural remains of Ireland are remarkable for their plain character, almost amounting to barrenness, yet to the thoughtful student they present many features of interest. Their simplicity of outline and fewness of parts give them a dignity peculiarly their own. With the English invasion we lose sight of the genuine Irish or Romanesque form of architecture, most of the details subsequent to that period following the transition in the English styles.'

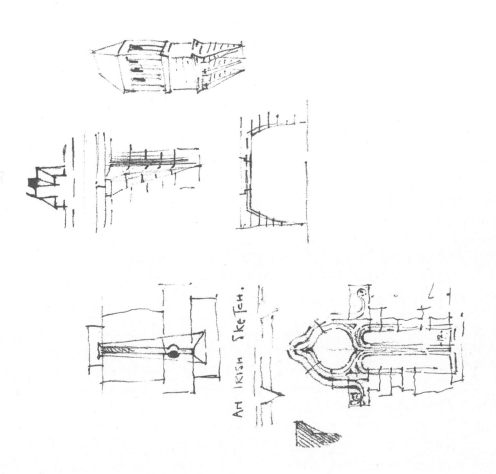

An Irish Sketch.

Plate 17

Inscribed: *Amisfield.   Tower.*

Amisfield Tower (c. 1600) in Dumfries and Galloway was cited by Mackintosh in his 'Scotch Baronial Architecture' lecture: 'The building affoards [sic] a fine and telling example of the love of corbelling so prevelent [sic] in the 4th period and is probably the most striking example of the adherence to the old Keep plan, while its external appearance is so entirely altered by the multiplicity of the turrets and ornaments piled up upon it as almost completely to conceal its origin.'[25]

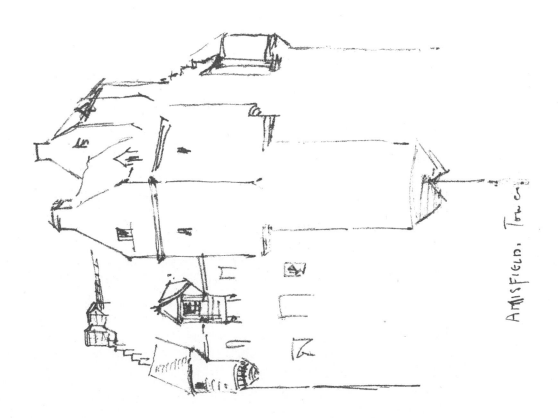

AMISFIELD. Tower

Plate 18

Inscribed: *Aldie Castle*

Aldie Castle (fourteenth to seventeenth centuries) in Perth and
Kinross, viewed from the southwest, is sketched with firm
graphic legibility, Mackintosh's focus being on the strong
architectural massing and the interlocking of its various parts.

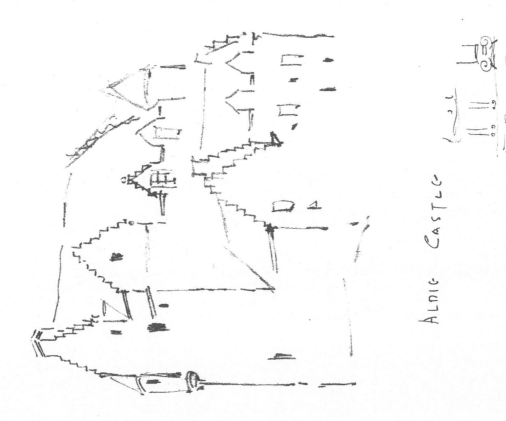

ALNIC CASTLE

Plate 19

Tomb of David Kyle, Abbey churchyard, Melrose

Inscribed: *Old Tomb Melrose Cornice. 12 Flutes. Base*

In the nineteenth century gravestone designs were part of an architect's stock-in-trade and Mackintosh may well have regarded such studies as a useful store of ideas. While exploring the pink and ochre-tinted stone ruins of the Cistercian Abbey at Melrose, he made this careful and measured study of the tomb of David Kyle in the graveyard near the south transept doorway.

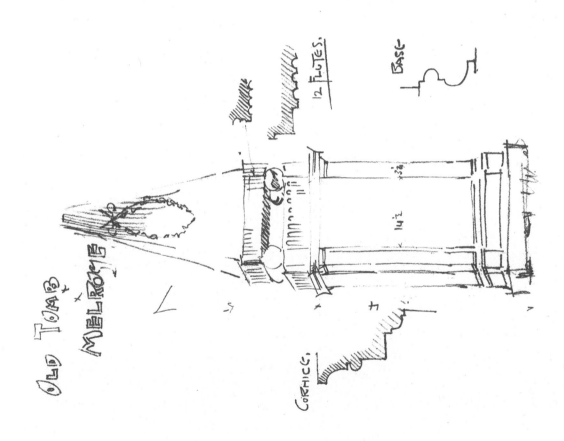

OLD TOMB
MELROSE

12 FLUTES.

BASE

CORNICE.

Plate 20

Towers and turrets were frequent features in late Victorian buildings. This page shows two examples. The upper motif, an octagonal tower, most likely Scottish and sketched before Mackintosh toured Italy, has not been identified. Similarities between the lower sketch and the tower of the Glasgow Herald Building (1893) suggest that this could have been preparatory work for that project.[26] One possibility is that, while working on the Herald Building, he recalled the tower he had sketched previously and its relevance to his current design problems, and that he then returned to this page and related his emerging design concept to the earlier drawing. His interest appears to be on the shifts in weight and mass of the tower as it rises, as he explores how the various structural shapes might be reconciled into an overall design.

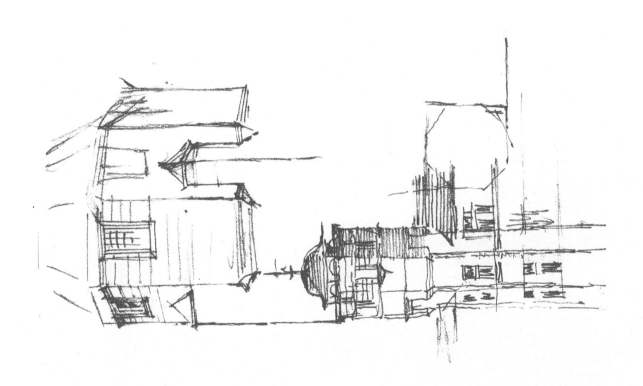

Plate 21

Inscribed and dated: *Panel and Doorhead, Brisbane Monument, Largs. Panel Mould. Jamb Mould. 17 May 1890*

Mackintosh mistakenly inscribed this gracefully sketched assembly of details. These belong to Skelmorlie Aisle (1636), Largs, Ayrshire.[27] The vaulted structure was the only remnant of Largs Parish Church, demolished in 1812, and contained the elaborate monument of Sir Robert Montgomerie. Here, Mackintosh sketched the intricately carved Montgomerie coat-of-arms situated above the door. His study of the vault and tomb continues over several further pages of the sketchbook. As with the tombs at Crail, the monument provided an interesting example of the use of imported patterns by seventeenth-century Scottish craftsmen.

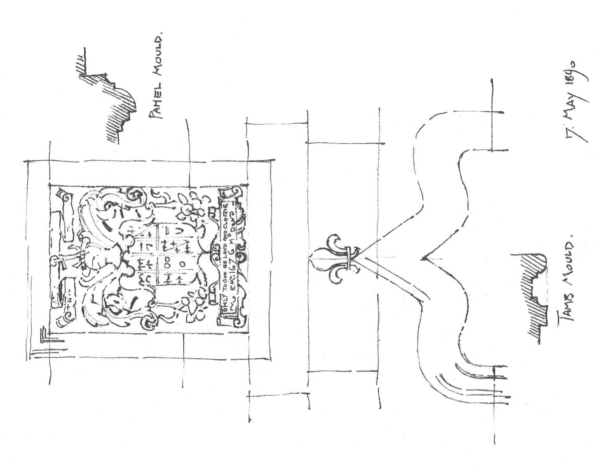

PANEL AND DOORHEAD, BRISBANE MONUMENT LARGS.

PANEL MOULD.

JAMB MOULD.

ONLY TO SIR THO LAND MACQUARIE
RX 167 GM POWE

7 MAY 189o

Plate 22

Alexander Thomson's Cairney Building, 40–42 Bath Street,
Glasgow (1861, demolished c. 1935)

This is one of Mackintosh's rare drawings of contemporary
architecture and, as he prepared his entry for the Thomson
Travelling Studentship, he may have had particular reasons for
sketching Thomson's design, the premises of the glass-stainer
John Cairney. In its balance and emphasis Mackintosh's study of
one bay of the building's elevation is markedly similar to an
illustration published in *Building News*, 31 May 1872. Yet, with
his office nearby on Bath Street, he would have been familiar
with the building itself.

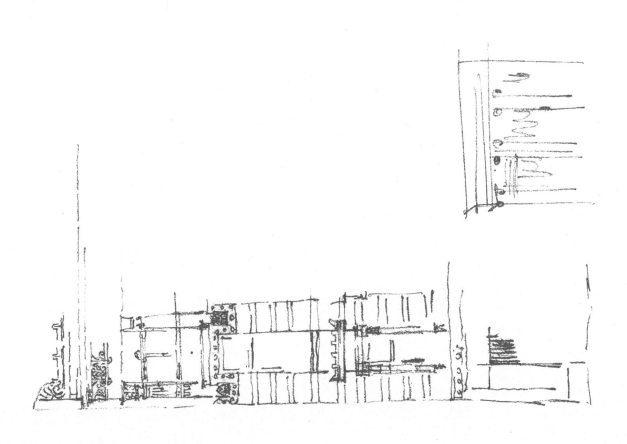

Plate 23

West tower, St Michael's, Linlithgow

In the Scottish sketchbook Mackintosh made various studies of St Michael's, Linlithgow. Here, in the sketchbook that was to accompany him to Italy, he drew the church's square west tower in a clear and emphatic hand that underlines the tower's solidity and structure.[28] His fascination with strong architectural forms, evident in his 'Scotch Baronial Architecture' lecture, would have transferred readily to the castles and fortifications of Italy.

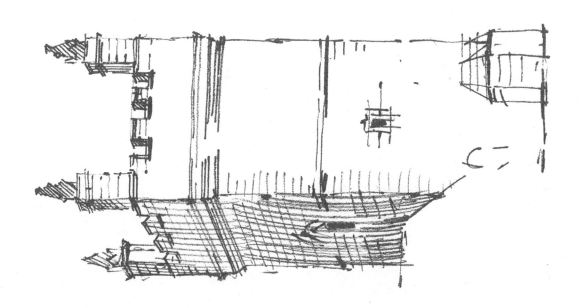

Plate 24

Inscribed: *Font Floor   San Miniato   Florence.*

The path to S. Miniato al Monte (begun eleventh century) was
Ruskin's favourite walk in Florence.[29] Mackintosh's diary entry
for 22 May records: 'went to S Miniato good way out but
worth going. Beautifully decorated roof. Fine mosaic floor, and
beautiful marbel [sic] screene [sic].' He sketched the intricate
geometric and figurative carpet-like pattern of the flooring in
the church's nave, a Byzantine-derived intarsia pavement dating
from 1207. Mackintosh selected the panel decorated with
twinned doves. Interestingly, he used bird names as competition
pseudonyms on several occasions, including the mythical 'Griffin'
for his Thomson Travelling Studentship entry.

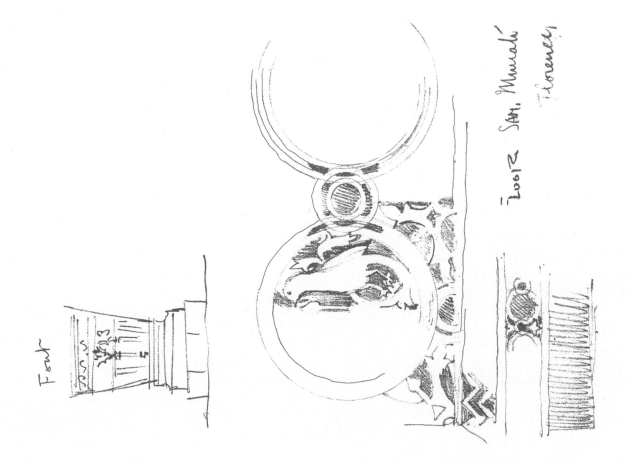

Font

Floor San. Miniata'
Firenze,

Plate 25

Campanile (begun fifteenth century, completed 1631) at
Church of S. Maria del Carmine (thirteenth century)

Inscribed: *Marina del Carmine Naples*
April 1890 [sic]

In Naples on 8 April 1891, his fourth day in Italy, Mackintosh
used this sketchbook for the first time there. He left a number
of pages blank before sketching the distinctive campanile
adjoining the right aisle of the church of S. Maria del Carmine.
In deft and fluid lines he registered the changing shapes of the
tower's upper stories, sketching only from where it rises above
the church roof. Despite the importance of the occasion and
his carefully stylish lettering, he misspelt the name and
mistakenly recorded the date as 1890.

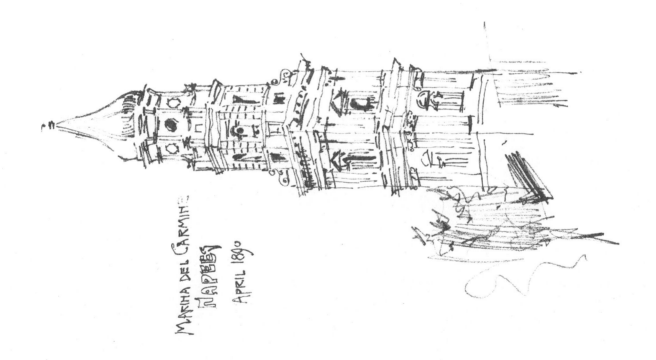

MARINA DEL CARMINE
NAPLES
APRIL 1890

Plate 26

Inscribed: *Monreale*

During his five days in Palermo, Mackintosh visited Monreale
twice. His diary entry for 14 April records a gasp of admiration
for the Cathedral's vast mosaic cycle and for the cloisters in the
nearby Benedictine Monastery, in particular its Romanesque
capitols: 'Some most beautifully carved caps. There are some
112 all round and they are all or nearly all different. Some of
them wonderfully good.' However, using this sketchbook for the
second time since arriving in Italy and here answering the
stipulations of his Studentship, it was one of the recycled
antique Corinthian capitols in the Cathedral's nave that became
his focus. The drawing is clear, exact and unhesitating. The curve
and volume of shaft and arch are cleverly indicated in a few
pencil strokes and the curling acanthus leaves suggested in
shorthand dots, dashes and shading. Interestingly, in this formal
architectural study he gives no hint of the rich mosaics covering
the high pulvin.

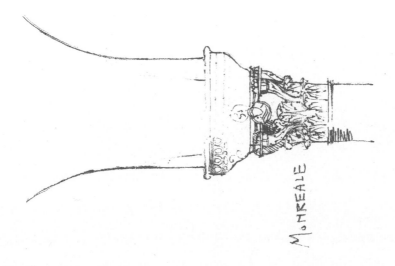

MONREALE

Plate 27

Sixteenth-century silk brocade of middle-eastern origin,
yellow and red on silver ground, still in Museo Nazionale del
Bargello, Florence

Inscribed: *Tapestry Florence   velvet pile National Museum Silver
ground.*

Mackintosh visited the Museo Nazionale del Bargello twice. On
one of those occasions he pencilled the outline of one section
of the pomegranate and winding foliage pattern on this rich
brocade, noting texture and colour. Either at the museum, or
perhaps afterwards in the quiet of his lodgings, he washed his
sketch with watercolour and used a brush in a calligraphy-like
inscription. This is one of only two coloured drawings in this
sketchbook. His response reflects Arts and Crafts sensibilities
and, with Glasgow an important centre of textile and carpet
manufacture, the strong emphasis on pattern design at the
School of Art. Throughout his career, Mackintosh designed
fabrics, from one-off stencil and needle-worked items to
commercial designs. Like this fragment, his designs were based
on conventionalized organic forms.

TAPESTRY
FLORENCE

NATIONAL MUSEUM
SILVER GROUND

Plate 28

Inscribed: *Porta del Popolo.   Rome.   Rome.   Florence*

Above: Porta del Popolo, Rome (1561) by Nani di Baccio Bigio, after a design by Michelangelo, modified in 1655 by Gianlorenzo Bernini (1598–1680) for a visit of Queen Christine of Sweden. It is interesting that Mackintosh, constantly wary of sham effects, should sketch a theatrical street screen by the master of Baroque.

Below left: the campanile (1163) of S. Francesca Romana (eighth century), also called S. Maria Nuova, built into the portico of the Temple of Venus and Rome in the Roman Forum.

Below right: in Florence, possibly at S. Lorenzo, Mackintosh returned to this page to sketch a classically proportioned pedimented door and its profile. The resulting page is a picturesque ensemble of Romanesque, Renaissance and Baroque motifs.

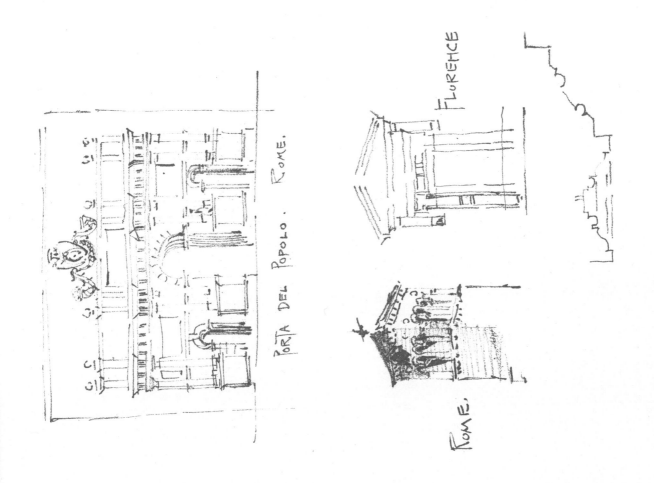

PORTA DEL POPOLO. ROME.

FLORENCE

ROME.

Plate 29

Inscribed: *Pal. Venezia.   Rome   Mosaic.   Door.   Florence.*

Above: Mackintosh used this page on two separate occasions. In Rome, he sketched the portal of the Palazzo Venezia (1455) by Giuliano da Maiano (1432–1490) and Leone Battista Alberti (1404–1472). Keen to remember the door's decorative moulding, he included a detailed study and profile to the side of his sketch.

Below: doors were clearly a conscious focus of Mackintosh's study and in Florence he returned to this page to record a further example.

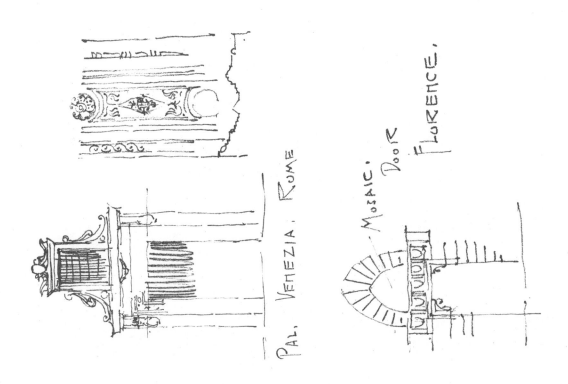

PAL. VENEZIA. ROME

MOSAIC.
DOOR
FLORENCE.

Plate 30

Inscribed: *Empoli.   Florence.*
Florentine   Chimney.   Dome   Florence

Below right: the eight-sided dome of S. Spirito by Filippo Brunelleschi
(1377–1446), completed posthumously in 1484, must have been of
considerable interest to the young architect. Brunelleschi's last great project, it
was the culmination of his experiences working on the cupola of the *Duomo*
and its masterful engineering was particularly admired by Anderson.[30]
Mackintosh's observations here may have contributed to his design for a
Chapter House (1892) and were perhaps remembered again in 1901 as he
worked on a domed concert hall for the Glasgow International Exhibition.
Above centre: the campanile attached to the sacristy at S. Spirito designed by
Baccio d'Agnolo (1462–1543).
Below left: a chimney in Florence, one of the few anonymous studies in the
sketchbook.
Above left: the upper part of the Torre di S. Agostino at S. Stefano degli
Agostiniani, Empoli (fourteenth to fifteenth centuries). The tower was
destroyed in 1944 but old photographs show it was among the tallest in the
small town. The Florence to Pisa train stopped at Empoli and it is possible that
while *en route* to Pisa, on the morning of 26 May, Mackintosh made this quick
thumbnail sketch from his train window.

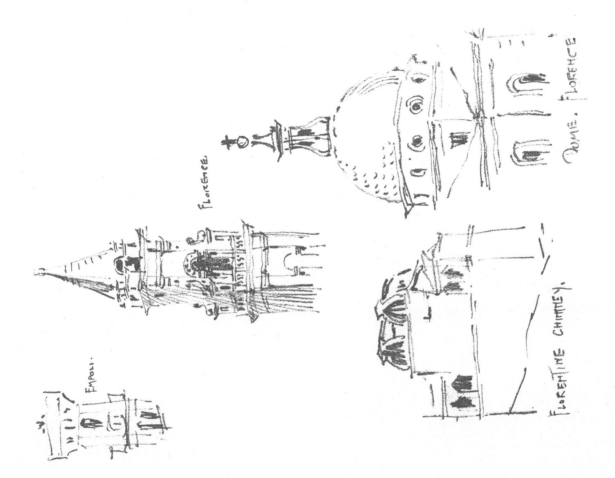

FLORENCE.

DUMO. FLORENCE.

FLORENTINE CHIMNEY.

EMPOLI.

Plate 31

Inscribed: *A Pallace [sic] Florence   S. Badia Florence.*
Della Robbia Panel   Dolphin Freeze [sic]   Pal. Vecchio Florence.

Left: most likely after his study of S. Spirito in Florence,
Mackintosh crossed the Piazza S. Spirito and turned the page of
his sketchbook to record the Palazzo Guadagni (1503–1506) by
Cronaca (Simone del Pollaiuolo, 1457–1508).
Above right: Renaissance portal (1495) of the Benedictine Abbey
(founded tenth century), Badia Fiorentina, Florence, by
Benedetto da Rovezzano. The enamelled terracotta tympanum
is by Benedetto Buglioni, in the manner of the della Robbia
studio.
Below right: Palazzo Vecchio (late thirteenth century) by Arnolfo
di Cambio (c.1245–c.1310). The 'Greek' Thomson scholar may
have remembered Ruskin's words as he sketched: 'I am much
inclined to love the vertical with a solemn frown of projection
(not a scowl) as in the Palazzo Vecchio of Florence. A mere
projecting shelf is not enough; the whole wall must, Jupiter-like,
nod as well as frown. Hence I think the propped Machicolations
of the Palazzo Vecchio and Duomo of Florence far grander
headings than any form of Greek cornice.'[31]

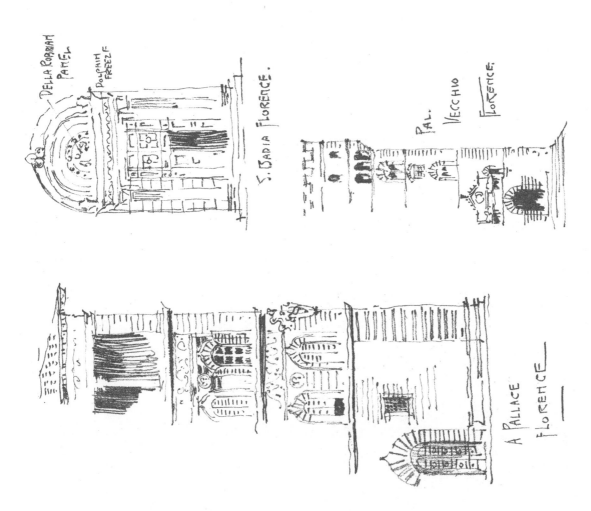

DELLA ROBBIAH PANEL

POLYPHIN FREEZE

S. BADIA FLORENCE.

PAL. VECCHIO FLORENCE.

A PALLACE FLORENCE

Plate 32

Palazzo Gianfigliazzi (begun thirteenth century), Via de Tornabuoni 1, Florence

Inscribed: *Florence*

The close fenestration and block-like strength of the city mansion of the Gianfigliazzi family, Via de Tornabuoni 1, Florence, must have held great appeal for Mackintosh. His hasty sketch would have served as a reminder of what he had studied: the rhythms of the façade, the deeply channelled and punctured stonework, heraldic plaques and deep cornice brackets. The patterns of fenestration on such older Florentine buildings may have informed his design for workmen's dwellings, submitted to the City of Glasgow Improvement Trust shortly after he returned from Italy.

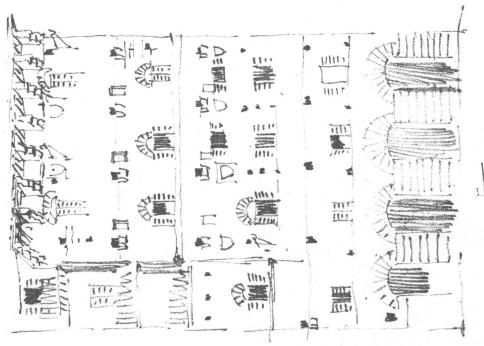

FLORENCE

Plate 33

Inscribed: *Florence. Door. Pallace [sic]*
Jamb. Window

Above left: a door at the Palazzo della Zecca (fourteenth century), Piazzale degli Uffizi, Florence. This building had been incorporated into the Uffizi in the sixteenth century and Mackintosh's selection indicates his particular taste. Ignoring the adjacent, more strident mannerist architecture of Vasari and Buontalenti, he focused on an older door, registering its wide, low proportions and the five heraldic shields on its architrave.
Above right: as if for comparison, here he selected the heavily rusticated, mannerist door of Palazzo di Bianca Cappello, Via Maggio (sixteenth century) designed by Bernardo Buontalenti (1531–1608).
Below left: the Palazzo Bartolini Salimbeni (1517–1520) by Baccio d'Agnolo. As with several other Florentine *palazzi* in this sketchbook, this was a hotel at the time of Mackintosh's visit.
Below right: the trabeated forms of classical architecture.

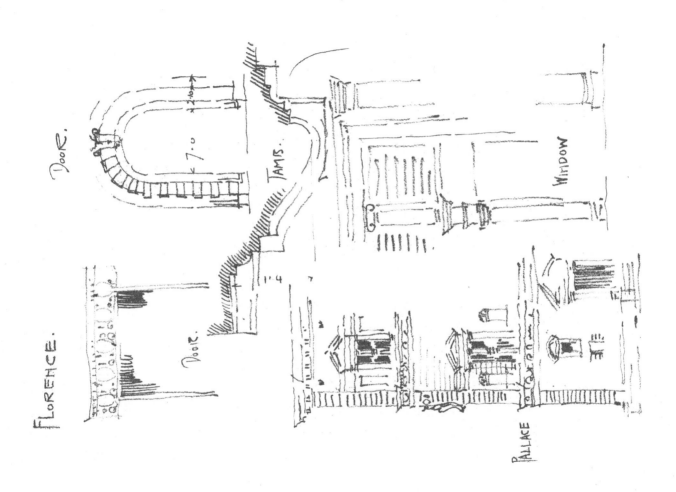

FLORENCE.

DOOR.

DOOR.

TAMIS.

7.0

2.10

1.4

WINDOW

PALLACE

Plate 34

Above: Palazzo Antinori (1461–1466), Via de Tornabuoni,
Florence, by Giuliano da Maiano after a design by Giuliano da
Sangallo (1445–1516). Beside his sketch of the elegant façade
Mackintosh added details of the dentilled cornice and the ovolo
moulding of the string course. He may have seen the
photograph, which W.J. Anderson later published with a
description of the Palazzo Antinori as a 'masterpiece of honest
simplicity'.[32]
Below: despite describing it in his diary, 20 May, as a 'bad tower,
crib from Siena', Mackintosh made a hasty sketch, his second
record of the Palazzo Vecchio.

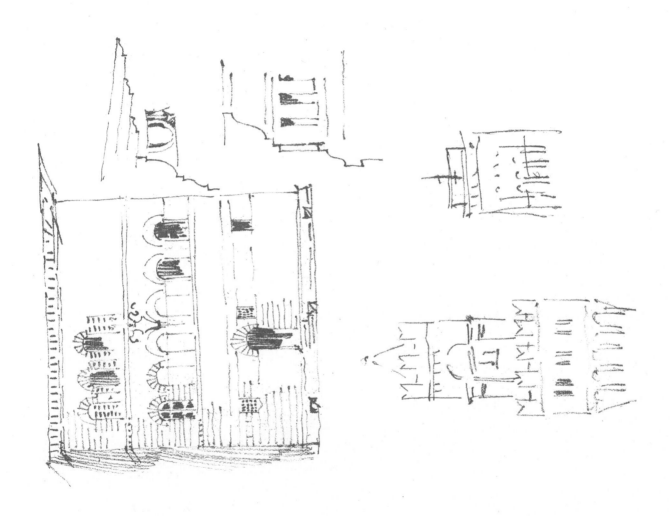

Plate 35

Inscribed: *Strings. Cornice Window Jamb*

Two pages of this sketchbook are devoted to studies of the Palazzo Strozzi (begun 1489) by Giuliano da Sangallo, Benedetto da Maiano (1442–1497) and Cronaca. Here, along with details of the large ovolos on the palace's celebrated cornice, he recorded other distinctive features: two profiles of the string course, both a side and frontal view of one of the giant brackets supporting the cornice, the masonry work of one of the windows and the Strozzi family's heraldic shield.

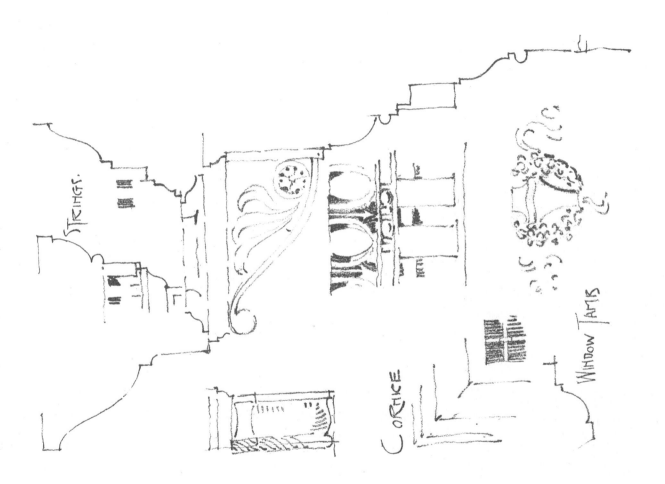

STRINGS.

CORNICE

WINDOW JAMB

Plate 36

Inscribed: *Museo National Florence.*
Baptistry. Rav.

Left: the massive, dark masonry and irregular window pattern of
the thirteenth-century Palazzo del Podesta, the Bargello or jail,
clearly appealed to Mackintosh. Interestingly, the Via Proconsolo,
where this sketch was made, was too narrow for him to have
observed the building as he sketched it. This image
demonstrates his remarkable capacity to manipulate forms and
extrapolate information from limited visual data, an ability later
evident in the sculptural multi-viewpoints and plasticity of his
designs.
Right: on 28 May Mackintosh arrived in Ravenna. There he
sketched the octagonal Baptistery of Bishop Neone (fifth
century), the oldest such structure in that town.

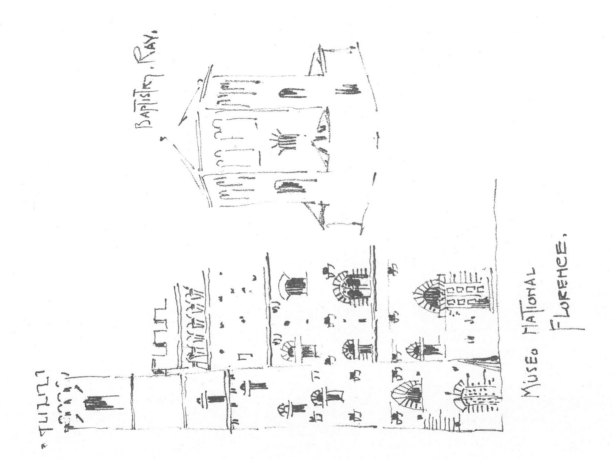

BAPTISTRY. RAV.

MUSEO NATIONAL
FLORENCE.

Plate 37

Inscribed: *Pisa.   P.al. Agostina   Pistoja*

Above: one bay of Pisa's most celebrated mansion, the *quattrocento* Palazzo Agostini and a study of a *piano nobile* window. Ruskin had made several sketches of the moulded terracotta foliage and medallions decorating the façade, the only remaining example in Pisa of this form of ornamentation. The Caffe dell'Ussero, a celebrated meeting place of the *Risorgimento*, still occupied the ground floor at the time of Mackintosh's visit.
Below left: the upper part of the campanile of Chiesa di S. Paolo (fourteenth century), Pistoia.
Below right: unidentified building and a chimney, typical of northern Italy.

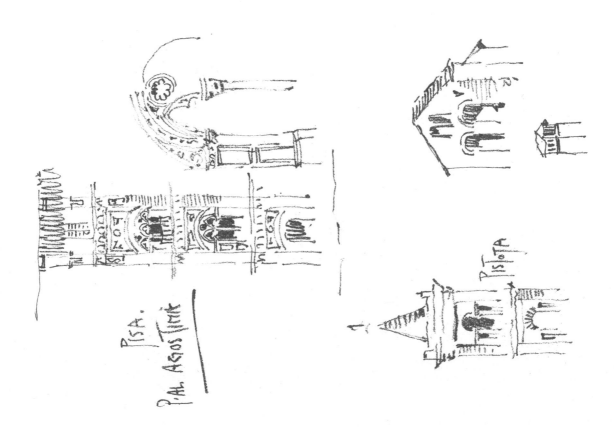

PISA.

P.AL. AGOSTINI

PISTOIA

Plate 38

Inscribed: *Mosaic Patern. [sic]*
Campo Santo. Pisa.   White marble   Red mosaic   Blue   Cap.

Above: Anderson described the Camposanto, Pisa, as a 'veritable museum'[33] and Mackintosh was clearly fascinated by the artefacts displayed there, filling three pages of his sketchbook. In 1888 this mosaic fragment had been sketched by Anderson. That published drawing had been copied by Mackintosh and the copy is found in the Dublin sketchbook of Scottish drawings.[34] On 26 May, in Pisa, he drew it again from life, noting its rich colour.

Below: some of the original Corinthian capitols from the façade of the *Duomo* were displayed in the Camposanto and Mackintosh made several studies of features normally too high above eye level for such close observation. The Camposanto was destroyed by incendiary bombs in 1944 and some of the items sketched there by Mackintosh are now in the Museo dell'Opera del Duomo, Pisa.

Mosaic Pattern · Campo Sant· Pisa·

white marble

Red marble

blue

Ex blue

CAP·

Plate 39

Inscribed: *Door   Pisa Cathedral
mosaic   Doorway Ravenna.*

Above: the bronze Porta di San Ranieri (1180) by Bonanno
Pisano on the south transept of the Cathedral was the only
original door to survive a fire in 1596. W.E. Nesfield's published
sketch of this door was, perhaps, known to Mackintosh.[35] In the
Campo dei Miracoli, Pisa, he provided himself with a brief 'note'.
The swirling lines and sharp dots of his pencil suggest the richly
carved architrave and capitols. The colourful mosaic voussoirs
were simply noted.
Below: one of two Renaissance doors by Giacomo Bianchi da
Venezia examined by Mackintosh in the museum at the Classe
Monastery. The elaborately carved sixteenth-century portal was
clearly of some interest to him and he included three details of
its ornamentation. This and its companion, also sketched by
Mackintosh,[36] are now in the *Primo Chiostro*, Museo Nazionale,
Ravenna.

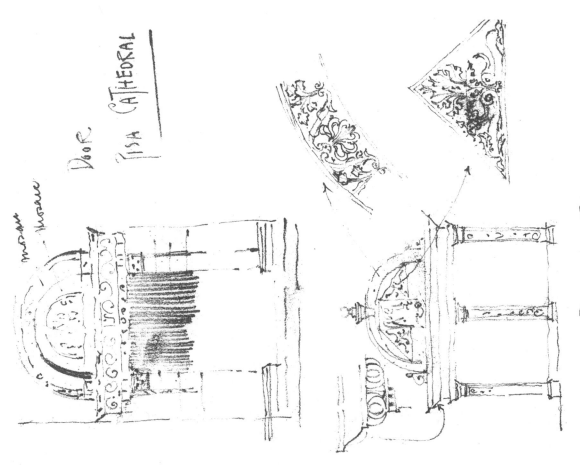

Door
Pisa Cathedral

Doorway Ravenna.

Plate 40

Inscribed: *Pal Comune. Pistoja*

Above: Mackintosh recorded just three of the five bays and a
few salient features, roof-tiles and corner shields, of Palazzo
degli Anziani, Pistoia, now Palazzo del Comune (late thirteenth
to fourteenth centuries). The mass and solidity of the building is
emphasized by this economy of detail and in the strong
hatching, suggestive of deep shadow beneath its arcade.
Below: this sketch does not appear to correspond to any
existing, or to any since destroyed or altered church complex in
Pistoia. Mackintosh's inscription may have been added later
from memory, but incorrectly.

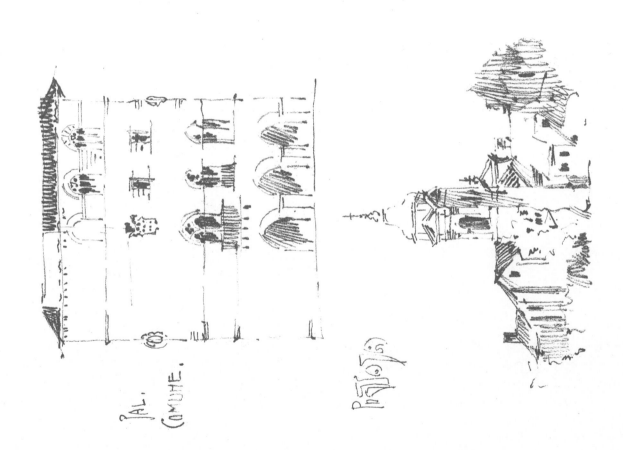

Plate 41

Inscribed: *Pistoja. S. Lorenzo*
Door   Ravenna

Left: mistakenly identified as 'S. Lorenzo', the Church of San
Giovanni Fuorcivitas (twelfth century) in Pistoia was admired
and photographed by Ruskin.[37] Mackintosh sketched one bay of
the banded green and white marble façade designed by
Gruamonte, that of the main entrance on Via Cavour. Blind
arcades and lozenge-shaped niches, suggested by clever pencil
shading, are typical of the richly decorative Pisan Romanesque
that he had disliked at Siena.
Above right: a thumbnail sketch showing barn-like buildings
suggests Mackintosh's sympathetic eye for vernacular
architecture.
Below right: Renaissance portal sketched at the monastery at
Classe, now in the *Primo Chiostro*, Museo Nazionale, Ravenna.[38]

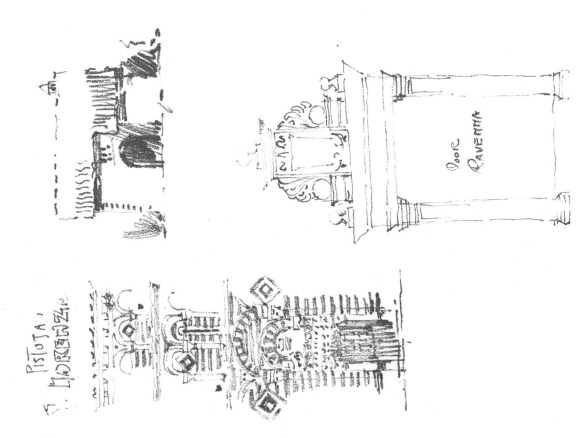

Door Ravenna

Pistoja.
S. Lorenzo.

Plate 42

Inscribed: *Duomo Bologna. Ravenna.*

Left: the campanile of the presbytery (thirteenth century), Cattedrale di San Pietro, Bologna, was sketched on 27 May. In his lecture Mackintosh echoed Ruskin by dismissing Bologna: 'I have very little to say of Bologna as we only stayed an afternoon there but what we did see was not calculated to keep us any longer.'[39]

Right: at Ravenna, he juxtaposed for comparison a second study, the upper part of the campanile (tenth century) at S. Giovanni Evangelista, the only square bell-tower in that city.

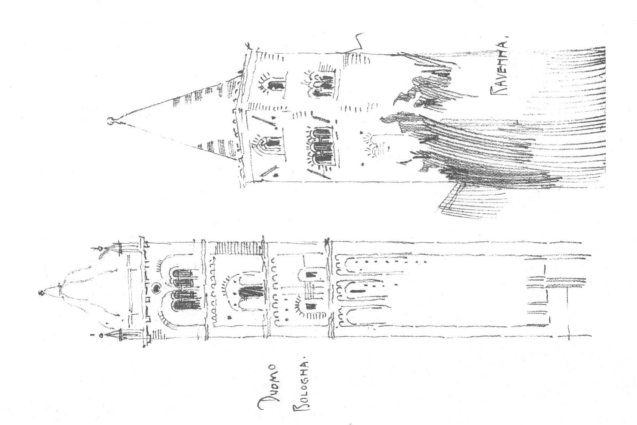

RAVENNA.

DUOMO
BOLOGNA.

Plate 43

Inscribed: *Pal. Scifamto [sic] Ferrara.*

Mackintosh sketched the entrance of Palazzo Schifanoia, the
summer residence of the d'Estes, on 1 June, misspelling its
name. The grandiose effect and rich ornamentation of this
monumental doorway, designed circa 1470 by Francesco del
Cossa, may have attracted him in being the only vertical feature
in an otherwise horizontal composition, the only elaboration on
an austere façade. His close interest in the richly carved
decoration is evident in three carefully observed studies.

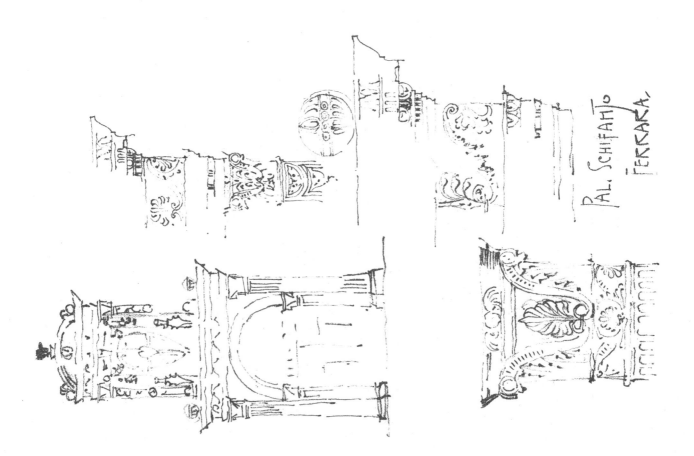

PAL. SCHIFANO
FERRARA.

Plate 44

Marble Transennae, twelfth century, Museo Arcivescovile, Ravenna

Inscribed: *Notes from Duomo Ravenna.*
Marble Frets.

Mackintosh's sharp eye perceived strong pattern in six fragments seen at the Museo Arcivescovile in Ravenna. The *transennae*, openwork lattice screens used in early Christian churches, had been part of the original *Duomo*, the Basilica Ursiana. Rescued from the ruins after an earthquake in 1733, they had been displayed in a museum at the nearby Archbishop's palace since the eighteenth century. The sharply defined patterns of void and mass, which translate in pencil to black and white, are intriguingly evocative of some of Mackintosh's use of negative space in his furniture designs.

NOTES FROM
DUOMO
RAVENNA.

Martin Pick.

Plate 45

Inscribed: *S. Vitale Ravenna.*

Above: the Basilica of S. Vitale (sixth century) is a complex mix
of classical and Byzantine influences. Mackintosh examined the
architectural massing closely and in this sketch sought an
understanding of the building's interlocking shapes and variously
angled roofs.
Below: he rarely drew figures but here, below the urban S.
Vitale, is a group of shawled peasants, seemingly approaching
the church across the flat plains of Emilia-Romagna. In creating
this picturesque composite image he was responding as an
artist as well as an architect and, for the second and last time in
this sketchbook, he used colour.

Plate 46

Inscribed: *S. Apollinaire in Classe. [sic] Ravenna.*

Mackintosh's pencil captures the impression of the church of S. Apollinare in Classe (sixth century) radiant in the bright sunlight of late spring.

S. APOLLINAIRE IN CLASSE, RAVENNA.

Plate 47

Inscribed: *Window Door. Well Head.*
Ferrara

Above left: a faint vertical line creates a composite image of the round-headed windows on the garden façade of the Palazzo Schifanoia. One half shows a plain and grilled ground-floor window. To the left of the dividing line is a first-floor window, dating from the palace's upward extension in the 1460s. The architect, Pietro Benvenuto degli Ordini, repeated the window's round-headed form but the more decorative terracotta surround reflects taste in a less defensive age.
Above right: the door at Via Voltapaletto 9, Ferrara.
Below left: like the church complex at Pistoia, this campanile has not been identified as any present, altered or destroyed building in Ferrara.
Below right: one of Ferrara's many wellheads.

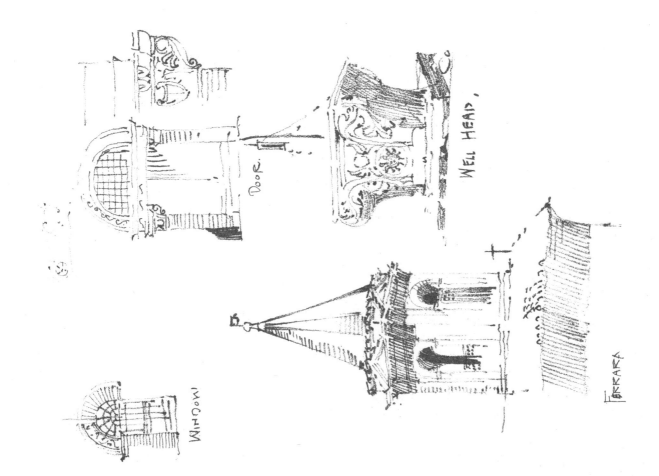

DOOR.

WELL HEAD,

WINDOW

FERRARA

Plate 48

Inscribed: *Castella Duchi Ferrara.*

The Castello Estense (late fourteenth century), designed by
Bartolino da Novara, dominates the centre of Ferrara. The
tower Mackintosh selected for this picturesque perspective was
not the oldest and most famous, the *Torre dei Leoni*, but that to
the southwest. The powerful massing of brick masonry, the
strong overhanging battlements, corbel projections and
defensive *avant-cours* stress the primarily military function of the
castle and must have appealed to his love for robust building.

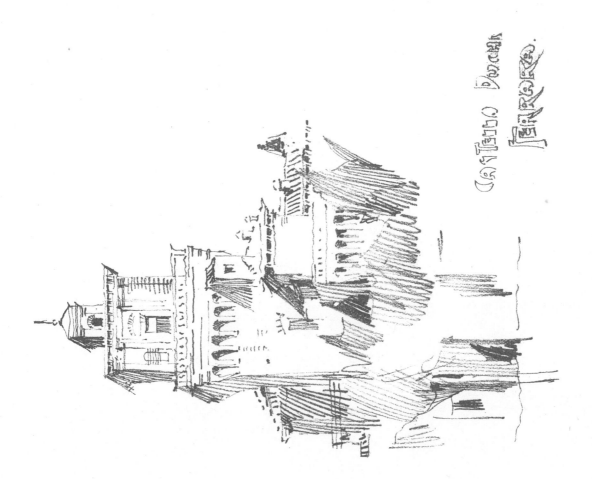

CASTELLO DUCALE
FERRARA.

Plate 49

Inscribed: *Doorway Ferrara. Same Round Door. Gondola Head.*

Above: the classically proportioned door of Largo Castello 20, Ferrara, and architrave profile. This large city mansion was once the Palazzo Del Monte di Pieta (1756–1761) and was a stock exchange and pawnshop at the time of Mackintosh's visit.
Below left: the brick campanile of S. Benedetto, Ferrara (fifteenth century) was unusual in northern Italy in being freestanding. The tower and much of the Benedictine monastery were destroyed during the Second World War and the present building is a 1950s reconstruction.
Below right: his reading of Ruskin prepared Mackintosh to respond sensually to the atmosphere of Venice.

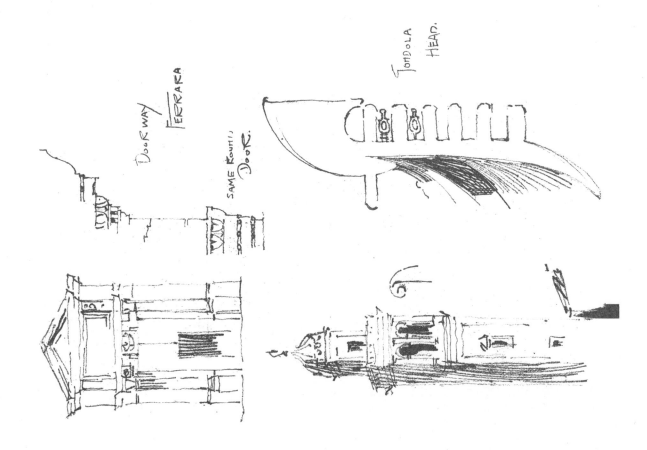

DOORWAY
FERRARA

SAME ROUND
DOOR.

GONDOLA
HEAD.

Plate 50

Above left: Dogana da Mar (1677–1678), by Guiseppe Benoni
Above right: Benedictine Abbey of S. Gregorio, ninth century,
rebuilt in fifteenth century

Inscribed: *Venice.*

One of the final drawings in the sketchbook is a collage created
at the southern entrance to the Grand Canal. Ignoring the
Baroque 'La Salute', Mackintosh sketched the buildings flanking
it: the maritime customs office and the apse of S. Gregorio.[40]
Sketched from the quay of the Zecca, or perhaps from a
gondola on the canal itself, he included impressions of the
water before him. His lecture notes call up such a scene: 'As
night approached another paradisical [sic] treat was given us.
Innumerable lights began to appear on the canal, every boat
had its lantern, and the gondolas moving rapidly along, were
followed by tracks of light which played and danced upon the
waters.'[41]

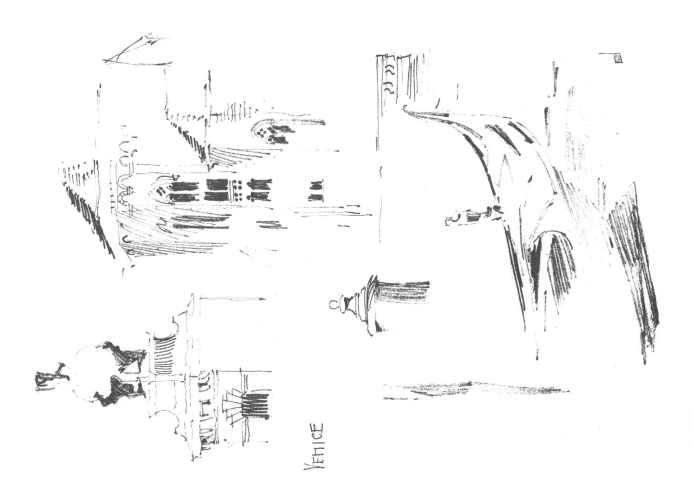

VENICE

Notes

1. Plate 16 taken from *Examples of Late Irish Architecture*. Drawn by J.L. Robinson. *Architect*, Vol. 18, 15 December 1877. A further page in the Italian sketchbook (2009 TX 20, N.L.I. not illustrated) is copied from the same volume: fountain at Cardiff Castle, designed by William Burges, *Architect*, 11 August 1877.

2. Phillips, G. (1840). *Architectural Ornament of all Nations*. London: Shaw & Sons. See Appendix I.

3. Mackintosh. Diary of an Italian Tour (5 April–7 July 1891) and A Tour in Italy (read to Glasgow Architectural Association (6 September 1892) and to Architectural Section of the Philosophical Society of Glasgow (28 November 1892)). In Robertson, P., editor (1990). *The Architectural Papers*, pp. 89–125.

4. Howarth, T. (1952). *Charles Rennie Mackintosh and the Modern Movement* (1st edition). London: Routledge & Kegan Paul, p. 9.

5. William James Anderson was President of the Glasgow Architectural Association. His admiration for Italian Renaissance architecture is evident in his published works, *Architectural Studies in Italy* (1890, Glasgow: Maclure, MacDonald & Co.) and *The Architecture of the Renaissance in Italy* (1896, London: B.T. Batsford).

6. Ruskin, J. (1886) *Seven Lamps of Architecture* (5th edition). London: George Allen (Chapter 'Beauty', para. xxi), p. 121.

7. Hare, A. (1883). *Cities of Southern Italy*. London: Smith & Elder, p. 6.

8. Robertson, P., editor (1990). *The Architectural Papers*. Wendlebury: White Cockade Publishing, p. 65.

9. Mackintosh (1891). Diary of an Italian Tour. In Robertson, P., editor (1990). *The Architectural Papers*. Wendlebury: White Cockade Publishing, p. 113.

10. Mackintosh's diary entry at Verona (12 June) notes 'J. Paxton and R. Dods left for Munich'. James Paxton was a fellow student of Mackintosh at the Glasgow School of Art (1886–1888). My thanks to George Rawson for this information. Robert Smith Dods (b. New Zealand 1868, d. Sydney, Australia 1920) trained in Edinburgh (1886–1890, ARIBA 1891). He toured Italy in 1891, returned to Australia in 1896 and practised in Brisbane until his death (obituary in *Builder*, 17 September 1920).

11. Ruskin, J. (1845). *Ruskin in Italy, Letters to his Parents*. H. Shapiro, editor (1972). Oxford Press, p. 118.

12. James, H. (1878). Recent Florence. *Architect*, Vol. 19, 18 May.

13. Mackintosh (1891). Correspondence relating to the Italian Tour. In Robertson, P., editor (1990). *The Architectural Papers*. Wendlebury: White Cockade Publishing, pp. 226–234.

14. Anderson, W.J. (1896). *The Architecture of the Renaissance in Italy*. London: B.T. Batsford. S. Spirito discussed as Brunelleschi's masterwork, pp. 17–18.

15. Mackintosh, op. cit., note 9, p. 109.

16. Ibid., p. 117.

17. Vatican, Biblioteca Apostolica, Barberini Codex.

18. Street, G.E. (1874). *Brick and Marble in the Middle Ages, Notes of tours in Northern Italy* (2nd edition). London: John Murray, pp. 388–89.

19. Mackintosh, op. cit., note 9, p. 115.

20. Crawford, A. (1995). *Charles Rennie Mackintosh*. London: Thames and Hudson Ltd., p. 18.

21. Sedding, J.D. (1893). Design. In Morris, W., editor, *Arts and Crafts Essays*. London: Rivington Percival & Co., p. 408.

22. Mackintosh (1925). Letter to F. Newbery, 28 December. Collection National Library of Scotland.

23. Webb, A. (1892). Review of Students' Work. Pugin Studentship and Institute Silver Medal. *Builder*, Vol. 62, 30 January, p. 81.

24. Kinchin, P. and Kinchin, J. (1988). *Glasgow's Great Exhibitions*. Wendlebury: White Cockade Publishing, p. 21.

25. Mackintosh (1891). Scotch Baronial Architecture. In Robertson, P., editor (1990). *The Architectural Papers*. Wendlebury: White Cockade Publishing, p. 60.

26. One of the final drawings in the Glasgow School of Art's

Italian sketchbook shows the Glasgow Herald Building as executed.

27. My thanks to Douglas Easton of the Largs & District Historical Society.

28. My thanks to Dr James MacAuley who identified this motif.

29. Ruskin, op. cit., note 11, p. 118.

30. Anderson, W.J. (1896). *The Architecture of the Renaissance in Italy.* London: B.T. Batsford, pp. 17–18.

31. Ruskin, op. cit., note 6 (Chapter 'Power', para. vii), p. 76.

32. Anderson, op. cit., note 14, pp. 21–22.

33. Anderson, W.J. (1890). *Architectural Studies in Italy.* Glasgow: Maclure, MacDonald & Co., plate IV.

34. See Chapter 2.

35. Nesfield, W.E. (1862). *Specimens of Medieval Architecture, Selected from Examples of the 12th and 13th Century in France, Italy and Norway.* London: Day & Son, plate V.

36. See Plate 41.

37. Ruskin Foundation, University of Lancaster. Collection, Daguerreotype (1845–1846).

38. See Plate 39.

39. Mackintosh, op. cit., note 9, p. 117.

40. My thanks to Signora Luisa Mutinelli.

41. Mackintosh, op. cit., note 9, p. 118.

THE BOTANICAL SKETCHBOOK

Mackintosh sketched flowers from an early age. While staying at Walberswick, Suffolk, in 1914–1915, the period of his best-known and most polished flower studies, he told the daughter of Francis Newbery that he had begun sketching them when he was 18 years old.[1] He also remembered that three of his earliest sketchbooks of flower drawings had been lost and it may well be that the sketchbook of botanical drawings, now in the National Library of Ireland, is one of those remembered, and missed, by Mackintosh. This sketchbook contains thirteen delicate and accurate pencil studies of commonly encountered cottage garden and wayside specimens.

From his early flower drawings to a desire to sit beneath a tree shortly before his death, Mackintosh showed a love of growing things. Plants were a constant joy, the cornerstone of his art and, after his career as an architect faltered, drawing and painting flowers became an important occupation and a consolation. During Mackintosh's student and early working years it was his habit to sketch vegetation in whichever sketchbook was at hand for architectural studies. The Dublin sketchbook of Scottish drawings contains such a page. However, the Dublin botanical sketchbook is the only known surviving sketchbook devoted exclusively to flowers. Not related directly to his profession, these flower studies were essentially private and recreational.

Inscriptions on some of these drawings, together with indications from nature's calendar, suggest that this sketchbook was used over a period of at least one year, being completed in late summer 1895. The years separating the Italian sketches and these flower drawings had been busy. Mackintosh had established himself in the offices of Honeyman and Keppie, entering competitions, studying and sketching. In the mid-1890s he was actively developing his architectural language on the Glasgow Herald Building

(1893–1896) and Queen Margaret Medical College (1894–1896). Decorative work, graphic and furniture designs were also absorbing his creative imagination. Also at this stage, and crucial to his development, he became more involved with art. From 1893 to 1896 a clique of students at the Glasgow School of Art assembled a number of hand-written collections of their work, which they called *The Magazine*. Several of Mackintosh's symbolic watercolours were included in these journals. While the symbolism of these works is enigmatic, the images employed are organic: eerily stylized plants, green shoots stirring secretly beneath the earth and strange amorphous growths.

In relation to the other Dublin sketchbooks it has been observed how Mackintosh's architectural drawings reflect many of the wider interests of his age as well as his own particular concerns. Those values and obsessions are no less evident in his flower studies. Two central preoccupations of

the maturing Mackintosh are demonstrated in the botanical sketchbook: the empirical naturalism of a scientific botanical illustrator and the pattern-seeking ideal of the designer. Basic to all his work was undoubtedly the love of and close familiarity with flowers he had learnt from his father, a keen gardener who had tended a large plot in the suburb of Dennistoun, fondly known to the family as the 'Garden of Eden'. McNair remembered Mackintosh as always on the lookout for flower specimens to sketch and study, occasionally climbing into gardens when a plant took his fancy.[2] Mackintosh was single-mindedly attentive to detail and his flower drawings may be seen as part of the tradition of botanical illustration. Indeed, it is believed that with the Walberswick floral studies he was working towards a complete collection of botanical illustrations for publication. Although sketched with subtle delicacy and despite a disregard for scale, with plants of all sizes similarly presented, the Dublin flower studies are drawn with remarkable precision and demonstrate concentrated and close observation. Botanical aspects are explored: the protective calyx, the corolla or petals and the inner whorl of stamen. Often a single species is isolated from its environment and shown without roots and from several viewpoints, a technique used in scientific botanical illustration.

However, the sketches reveal something more than a deep personal response to nature and its careful and correct reproduction. Macintosh shared the late Victorian preoccupation with the search for a new, ahistoric aesthetic. The concept of nature as the fountainhead of flexible, functional and primarily beautiful ideas preoccupied designers, pattern makers and philosophers of the nineteenth century. That precept was strongly advocated by Ruskin and explicitly articulated by C.F.A. Voysey (1857–1941): 'Go to nature directly for inspiration and guidance.'[3] Such an approach was central to Mackintosh. Much of his architectural and design vocabulary was based upon nature, the structure of root and branch, patterns of leaf, bud and bloom. His flower drawings may be seen as part of a 'quasi-scientific method of invention',[4] with Mackintosh extracting design principles from the sinuous curves of leaves and the verticals of stems. With nature as his blueprint, these flower drawings are at the very root of his thinking. Organic forms explored in his private sketches find a reflection in much of his subsequent design: high-backed chairs seeming to seek the light like sunflowers, the steel beams in the basement of the Glasgow School of Art that bend and twist like a giant root system, the complex curves and vegetable shapes of his wrought-iron work and in much of the stencil work at Miss Cranston's tea-rooms and Hill House. Flowers were the basis for his textile designs of the 1920s.

After the publication of Howarth's monograph in 1952, Dr Farmer, the then owner of the sketchbooks, recognized the aptness of a description of Mackintosh's early flower drawings and its relevance to the drawings in his possession. He copied the following passage onto the flyleaf of this sketchbook.

> _Charles Rennie Mackintosh and_
> _The Modern Movement (1952), 197._ [sic]
> 'Those lovely lace-like drawings
> – Japanese in character – ...
> reveal a highly developped [sic] faculty
> for precise observation of detail
> and a complete understanding of
> structural form.'[5]

These words encapsulate several essential aspects of the drawings: the influence of Japan and precise botanical detail coupled with the imposition of a formal design structure.

Mackintosh shared the period's fascination with Japanese art,[6] the impact of which is evident in the _Japonisme_ of Aubrey Beardsley, James McNeill Whistler and in the Aesthetic Movement. For architects and designers, the numerous articles on Japanese aesthetics featured in contemporary journals and descriptions by writers such as Christopher Dresser provided a glimpse of an alternative ideal. The drawings in this sketchbook show a Japanese-like restraint and understatement in capturing organic essentials. Flowers are delicate yet strong, composed in the carefully balanced asymmetry, the quiet harmonies and timelessness of _ikenobo_, the Japanese art of flower drawing. Just as Japanese art stresses linear rather than tonal values, Mackintosh's lines are deceptively simple and floating shapes are used to accentuate floral structure without fussiness or shading.

Another contemporary influence evident is the _fin-de-siècle_ pantheistic mysticism, epitomized in the Celtic Revival and reflected in literature of the period: Sir James Frazer's _The Golden Bough_ (12 vols, 1890–1915) and the short-lived quarterly review, *Evergreen* (1895–1897) edited by Sir Patrick Geddes. This mood finds an echo in the sacramental reverence pervading Mackintosh's transcendental approach to nature. His flower studies give no hint of movement. Apparently sketched quickly *en plein air*, the plants are, nonetheless, supernaturally still, with straight unswaying stems and unruffled petals. This transcendence was explicitly articulated some years later when, in his lecture 'Seemliness' (1902), he stated: 'Art is the Flower, Life is the Green Leaf'.[7] Thus, for Mackintosh the flower was an allegory for art, the highest of man's achievements.

The lecture 'Seemliness' also makes it clear that, for Mackintosh, art and life were inextricably bound. Perhaps, more than his building studies, the private flower drawings are personally revealing and should be seen in the context of his emotional development. The mid-1890s were salad days for the young man. He had the close friendship of Herbert McNair. Through classes at the School of Art

the two young architects came into contact with a group of intelligent and active young fellow students, including a number of women. The circle of friends included John Keppie's sister, Jessie, to whom Mackintosh was informally engaged. The group also included the Macdonald sisters, Margaret (1864–1933) and Frances (1873-1921). Together with Herbert McNair, Mackintosh and the Macdonalds began a period of collaborative design and exhibiting, becoming known as 'the Four'. The wider circle of friends called themselves 'the Immortals', suggesting feelings of confident invincibility and a total optimism in their prospects and abilities. At weekends 'the Immortals' gathered in Prestwick, Ayrshire, where John Keppie had a holiday home. To supplement the accommodation two bungalows were rented a few miles away, near Dunure. These were christened 'the Roaring Camp', giving some indication of unrestrained high spirits. Playfulness and lively good humour was evidently the mood of these gatherings.[8] Several of the Dublin sketches were made at nearby West Kilbride and on the Isle of Bute and it seems likely that it was on such occasions that at least some of these flower sketches were created.

The mid-1890s may also be seen as a watershed period of choice and change for Mackintosh, both professionally and personally. In 1895 McNair left the offices of Honeyman and Keppie to establish an independent design studio. With the other two members of 'the Four', the Macdonald sisters, also designing independently, Macintosh may have felt unsettled. In 1895, he too rented his own studio. The significance of his self-consciously artistic dress at this period has been pointed out.[9] His symbolic paintings, *The Tree of Influence* and *The Tree of Personal Effort* (Glasgow School of Art, 1895) are also suggestive of a period of uncertainty in his ambitions and direction. Thus, these flower sketches may be contemporaneous with a decision to pursue art and design rather than a purely commercial architecture, to work close to his principles rather than to seek conventional success.

At about the same time, the year of this sketchbook, Mackintosh took the drastic step, in terms of Victorian social mores, of breaking his understanding with Jessie Keppie. He presented her with a parting gift, a casket filled with half-formed desiccated rose buds and symbolically decorated with stunted and immature plant-forms (Victoria and Albert Museum). An arresting aspect of the flower drawings, made in what must have been a turbulent year in his emotional life, is the strong symbolism of sexuality and of blossoming love. Many of these flowers have the erotic charge of fecundity, the subliminal sensuality of ripe and revealingly open blossoms, often laden with seedpods or fruits. One page in particular is perhaps a silent witness to a turning point in his relationship with Margaret Macdonald, who became his wife in 1900 and remained his life-long love, muse and mainstay (Plate 56). In the drawing of the flower monkshood the initials 'MM' are buried within the stem of the central bloom. This was perhaps the first time Mackintosh placed her initials on one of his works, a practice that became common after their marriage. The flower, strangely evocative of the smooth swelling of Margaret's own hair, is like the presentation of a bouquet, as conscious a declaration of love as the carving of lovers' initials on the bark of a tree. This symbolic announcement of the bans is not only an offering of love, but also recognition of the central role Margaret played in his creative life. The letters, one above the other, are so placed that their sides are aligned with the walls of the flower-stem and the Ms, like two tiny valves, seem to control the flow of sap. Towards the end of his life Mackintosh wrote in a letter to Margaret: 'any one who can read their meaning would find only three words "I love you". Good night M M perhaps

you can read the three words and perhaps they will mean something to you.'[10] This sketch marks the beginning of that relationship, which was central to his creativity.

It is against that background, a time of highest artistic hope and spiritual belonging, of crisis and resolution, that Mackintosh completed this sketchbook. The final drawing, and the last of the Dublin collection, shows the transparent seed-pocket of the flower honesty, appropriately symbolic of the revealing nature of these works. He left the last few pages unused and put the sketchbook aside. Ahead of him was the most creative and professionally active decade of his career: the satisfaction of creating his masterwork, the Glasgow School of Art (1896–1909), the triumphs of the Vienna and the Turin Exhibitions (1900 and 1902) and the fulfilment of working for sympathetic clients such as Miss Cranston and Walter Blackie. Ahead of him also were the later years of disappointment and isolation.

Plate 51

Mackintosh apparently used this page on two separate
occasions. Above, and seemingly sketched first, is an intimate
frontal view of an orchid, probably *Cymbidium*.[11] These hothouse
or indoor plants bloom in February or March and were popular
in Victorian winter-gardens. The petals on this specimen already
appear to curl and wilt, somehow suggesting that Mackintosh
might have observed it in a corsage. Beneath, at an early stage
of development and with corolla just beginning to unfurl, is a
drawing apparently added at a later stage, possibly a single
inflorescence of the summer-flowering delphinium. The
diminutive cartouche, a feature Mackintosh derived from
Japanese prints, is empty here. The cartouche became one of
Mackintosh's favourite ways of locating inscriptions and, in his
best-known flower studies made at Walberswick in 1914 and
1915, it often contained the initials of his wife Margaret along
with his own.

Plate 52

The hardy perennial *Antirrhinum majus,* commonly called snapdragon, flowers from July to October and, along with the study of delphinium on the previous page, may have been sketched in summer 1894. While the original subject remains identifiable, Mackintosh explores the flower's structure and his study is a pattern-seeking distillation. A stylized bloom is transmuted to an almost symmetrical abstraction as the flower is deconstructed. By isolating certain shapes and revolving perspectives, the flower's form is conventionalized and new patterns are generated.

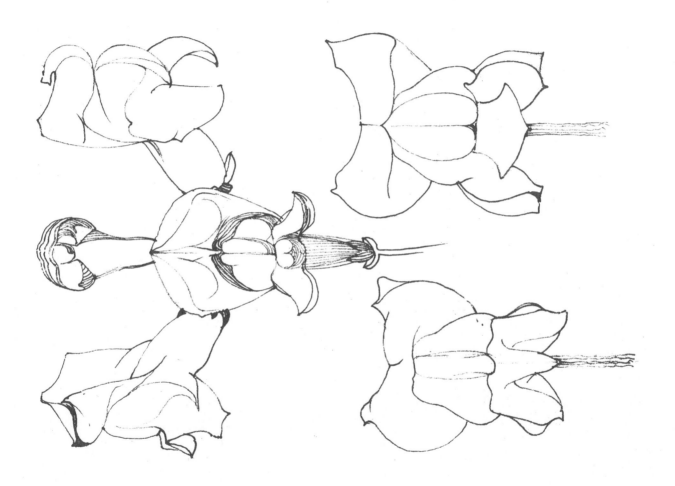

Plate 53

Inscribed: *Chrismas Rose. [sic]*

Helleborus niger, called the Christmas rose because of its winter blooms, was possibly sketched in winter 1894/1895. The bowl-shaped flowers are drawn from several viewpoints and at different stages of their lifecycle, a technique used in *Ikebana*, the Japanese art of flower arranging.[12] One formalized flower is shown in highly structured architectonic plan, its five perfect petals spreading from its seed-centre. Two semi-closed flowers and a ripe seed-head overlap, partly superimposed on each other, lending vitality to this otherwise highly structured study. Twenty years later, at Walberswick, Mackintosh again drew the hellebore (Victoria and Albert Museum, 1915).

CHRISMAS ROSE.

Plate 54

Inscribed: *Goosberry Flower [sic]   Currant.   Glasgow.*

The leaf and blossom of the gooseberry bush, which flowers in April, were possibly sketched in spring 1895. Essential characteristics are indicated with a frothy vitality and without obsessive detailing. Mackintosh may have been attracted to the gooseberry as a symbol of potentiality and fresh beginnings. In the second issue of the student review of the Glasgow School of Art, *The Magazine*, Mackintosh included a watercolour, *Cabbages in an Orchard* (Glasgow School of Art). The accompanying text berates those who fail to value the simple, the 'Common or Garden Cabbage'. Mackintosh ends enigmatically: 'anything in the sketch you cannot call a tree or a cabbage – call a gooseberry bush'.[13]

CURRANT.

GLASGOW.

FLOWER

GOOSEBERRY

Plate 55

Inscribed: *Ascog   May 1895.*

The Isle of Bute off the Ayrshire coast was, from the 1860s, easily reached from Glasgow by rail and ferry. Ascog, little more than a small shore-side chapel and some villas, is a few kilometres south of the island's ferry terminus at Rothesay. This sketch may represent the small, delicate flowers of *Saponaria*, commonly called rock soapwort. Mackintosh has conventionalized the flower by an elegant elongation of its stems. This approach is also seen in the pattern-like shading. In the mid-1890s Mackintosh was consciously developing his own calligraphic style and here he combines vertical and horizontal lettering.

Plate 56

Inscribed: *WK.   July 1895. MM H.M.   J.F.   CB*

This highly personal and significant sketch of the flower
Aconitum napellus, commonly called monkshood, a poisonous
summer-flowering herbaceous perennial, was made at West
Kilbride in Ayrshire. The initials of Margaret Macdonald, buried
within the flower's stem, is possibly the first instance Mackintosh
joined her name to his in this way. After their marriage in 1900,
this became customary whenever she was present as he
sketched. As if to curb the audacity of his open courtship,
Mackintosh included the initials of others, chaperones or
witnesses as it were. 'H.M.' is probably Herbert McNair,
Mackintosh's closest male friend of the period. The identity of
others may only be guessed at. However, it seems likely they
were intimate friends and 'Immortals'.

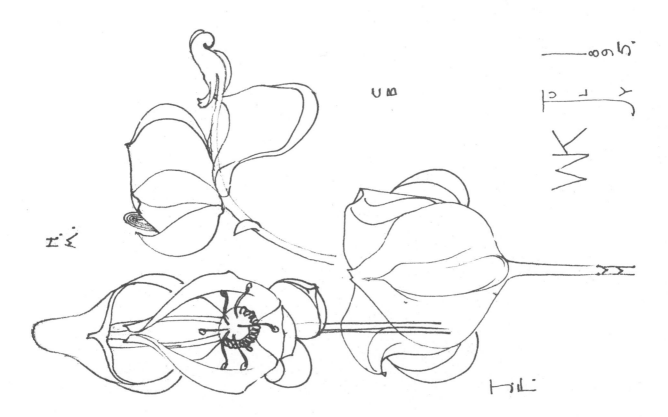

Plate 57

Inscribed: *Candytuft. Patati.   W Kilbride.*

This page illustrates two flower types. *Iberis sempervirens*, commonly called candytuft, is a low-growing Alpine that flowers in July and August. Mackintosh's close study shows the reproductive centre of the tiny flower, the carpel and stamen. Beneath is the flower of the potato plant, stylized and shown from several viewpoints, including an unusual rear view.

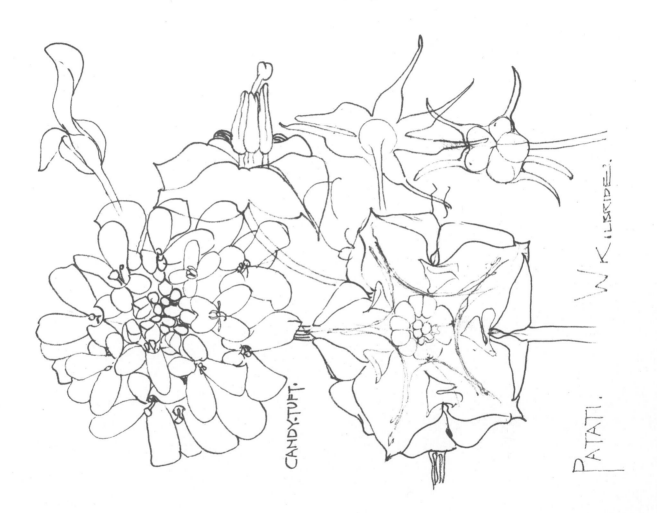

CANDY-TUFT.

PATATI.   W KILBRIDE.

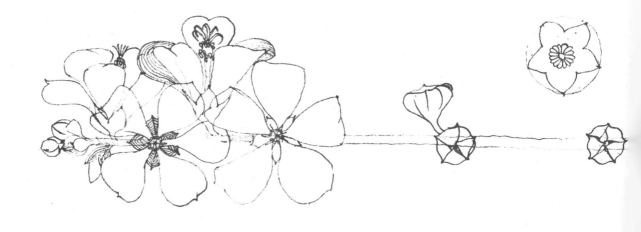

WK. 1895

Plate 58 *(previous pages)*

Inscribed: *WK.   1895*

Sketched at West Kilbride, the tall spires of *Althaea rosea*, or
hollyhock, are quintessential cottage-garden flowers and the
symbol of ambition and fecundity. The hollyhock blooms in mid
to late summer and this flower was already past its first flush
when Mackintosh sketched it, with seed pods fully formed on
the lower stem. Two isolated blooms are shown, one a tight
bud just beginning to unfurl from the calyx, the other a stylized
bloom viewed in plan and distilled to geometric shapes. The
drawing crosses the sketchbook's spine, accentuating the
slender verticality. This striking exaggeration reflects
Mackintosh's tendency to attenuate form, notably in his chair
designs.

Plate 59 *(following pages)*

Inscribed: *Birds Eye View [sic] Plan Looking Down. Orange Lily Bud and Stem. All Green.*

This trumpet-shaped member of the lily family blooms in mid to late summer. An unbending and attenuated stem, almost leafless, crosses two pages. The vertical formality and abstraction of the plant is emphasized in stylish lettering. A certain austerity is relieved by a charming graphic whimsy, a tiny spider. Perhaps Mackintosh sketched a real insect spinning its web among the flowers. Writing to Margaret in 1927 he explicitly points to such an incident. 'The last three mornings my drawings have been covered with all sorts of insects which I have to brush aside – the ones I don't hurt are innumerable small red spiders – they are all over my drawing because I am still hoping they indicate luck although I know they can't bring luck.'[14]

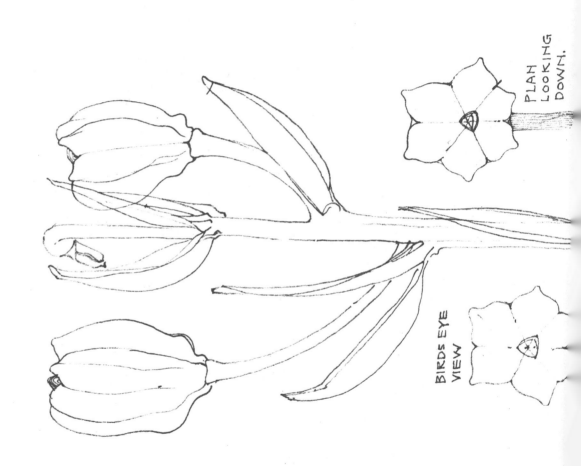

PLAN
LOOKING
DOWN.

BIRDS EYE
VIEW

ORANGE ↓ BUD AND STEM.

ALL GREEN.

Plate 60

Inscribed: *Honesty.   Seed   W.K.   1895.*

Sprays of *Lunaria*, commonly called honesty, are ubiquitous in
dried flower arrangements. However, it was Mackintosh's habit
to draw living plants. Honesty blooms between April and June
and seeds in August and September and, at West Kilbride,
Mackintosh most likely sketched a growing plant in late summer
1895. He concentrated on the transparent disk-shaped seed-
heads, so clearly defined as to suggest they were viewed against
strong light. Honesty may have had a particular resonance for
Mackintosh. Among his adaptations of its form in his design
work is a conventionalized honesty seed in the glass panel of
the Director's office, Glasgow School of Art.

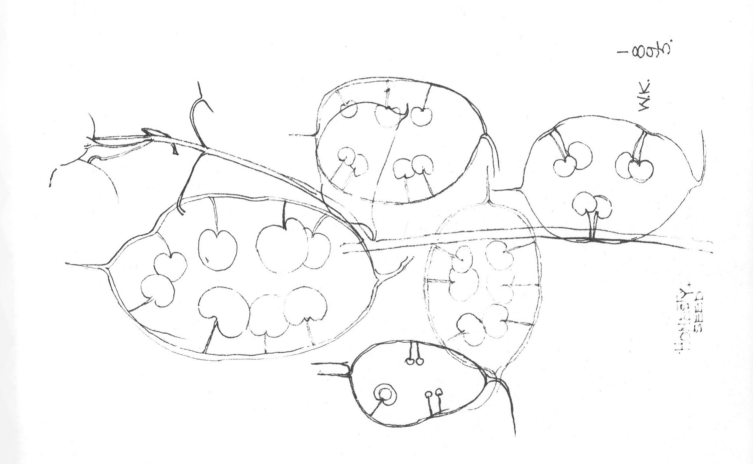

Notes

1. Sturrock, M. (August 1973). *Connoisseur*, Vol. 183, p. 287. Also published in Moffat, A. (1989). *Remembering Charles Rennie Mackintosh: An Illustrated Biography*, p. 79.

2. Howarth, T. (1977). *Charles Rennie Mackintosh and the Modern Movement*. London: Routledge & Kegan Paul, p. 7.

3. Voysey, C.F.A. (September 1893). *The Studio*, Vol. 1, No. 6, p. 234.

4. Brett, D. (1992). *Charles Rennie Mackintosh, The Poetics of Workmanship*. London: Reaktion, p. 72.

5. Howarth, T. (1952). *Charles Rennie Mackintosh and the Modern Movement* (1st edition). London: Routledge & Kegan Paul, p. 197.

6. See Buchanan, W. (spring 1980). Japanese Influences on Charles Rennie Mackintosh. *CRM Society Newsletter*, Vol. 25, pp. 3–6.

7. Mackintosh. (1902). Seemliness. In Robertson, P., editor (1990). *The Architectural Papers*. Wendlebury: White Cockade Publishing, p. 224.

8. See Rawson, G. (summer 1993). Mackintosh, Jessie Keppie and the Immortals, some new material. *CRM Society Newsletter*, Vol. 62, pp. 4–6.

9. Crawford, A. (1995). *Charles Rennie Mackintosh*. London: Thames and Hudson Ltd, p. 24.

10. Mackintosh. In Robertson, P., editor (2001). *The Chronycle, Letters of C.R. Mackintosh to Margaret Macdonald Mackintosh*. Glasgow: Hunterian Art Gallery, p. 72.

11. My thanks to Dr Matthew Jebb, National Botanic Gardens, Dublin, for comments and advice.

12. In 1891 the first book on *Ikebana* by a westerner was published: *Floral Art of Japan* by Josiah Conder.

13. Mackintosh. (April 1894). *Cabbages in an Orchard. The Magazine*. Collection Glasgow School of Art.

14. Mackintosh. Op. cit., note 10, p. 100.

APPENDIX I

Mackintosh's book list contained in the sketchbook of Italian drawings

The final page of the Italian sketchbook contains a book list in Mackintosh's hand. The reference numbers recorded are those still used for older books at the Mitchell Library, Glasgow. For the ambitious and hard-working student, the library, founded in 1877, provided an invaluable resource free of charge. In May 1890 the library closed its Ingram Street premises and remained closed to the public until October 1891 while stocks were removed to a new location on Millar Street. The *Architect* commented on the considerable inconvenience to the public[1] and for Mackintosh, this coincided with a key period of preparation for his Italian tour.

The list indicates a serious approach to his studies on the part of Mackintosh. The oldest item is the Earl of Aberdeen's polemic on Grecian aesthetics, first published in 1822. Other, more up-to-date, publications show his awareness of current reference works: for example, MacGibbon and Ross, published in five volumes between 1887 and 1892. With certain items acquired by the Mitchell Library only in 1888, namely *Architecture of France and Italy* by Richard Rowand Anderson and *Architectural Ornament of all Nations* by George Phillips, it seems that this list was assembled between 1888 and the early 1890s.

The following is Mackintosh's list. He omitted publication and, in some cases, author details. These are added here within square brackets. Mackintosh's own words are presented in italics.

D.14119	*Viollet-le-Duc, Dictionnaire Raisonné de l'Architecture Française.* [(1873). Paris: A. Morel & Co.]
D.43378	*Habitations of Man in all Ages.* [Viollet-le-Duc, Eugene-Emanuel. (1876). Translated by Benjamin Bucknall. London: Sampson Low, Marston Searle & Rivington.]
D.91323	*White, Architecture and Public Buildings in London and Paris.* [White, William H. (1884). London: P.S. King & Sons.]
D.120349	*Anderson, Architecture of France and Italy.* [Examples of the Municipal, Commercial and Street Architecture of France and Italy from the 12th to 15th century, measured and drawn by R. Anderson, Architect, Edinburgh, (1868). Edinburgh & Glasgow: W. Mackenzie. The reputation of the author, Sir Robert Rowand Anderson (1834–1921), founder of the National Art Survey and one of Edinburgh's most distinguished architects, would have been known to Mackintosh.]
D.120347	*Architectural Ornament of all Nations.* [Phillips, George. (1840). London: Shaw & Sons.]
D.5622	*Earl of Aberdeen, Principals* [sic] *of Beauty in Grecian Architecture.* [George, Earl of

Aberdeen (1st edition 1822). *An Inquiry into the Principles of Beauty in Grecian Architecture,* London: John Weale.]

D.13410   *-do-* [Ibid. 2nd edition, 1860.]

D.97939   *McGibbon and Ross, Arch. of Scotland.* [MacGibbon, David and Ross, Thomas. (Vol. I & II, 1887. Vol. III, 1889. Vol. IV & V, 1892). *The Castellated and Domestic Architecture of Scotland,* Edinburgh: David Douglas.]

D.28951   *British Architect from 1877–1880.*

D.28999   *The Architect from 1877.*

Note

1. The Mitchell Library (1892). *Architect,* Vol. 48, 16 September, p. 184.

APPENDIX II

A chronology of Mackintosh's Italian journey, 1891

5–12 April	Naples. Visited Pompeii on 5, 7 and 9 April.
13–18 April	Palermo. Visited Monreale on 14 and 16 April.
19 April – 4 May	Rome.
4–10 May	Orvieto.
10–19 May	Siena.
19–26 May	Florence.
26 May	Pisa.
27 May	Pistoia and Bologna.
27 May – 1 June	Ravenna.
1 June	Ferrara.
1–10 June	Venice. On 7 June Mackintosh celebrated his 23rd birthday. During his stay in Venice he reached the final pages of the Dublin Italian sketchbook and the record of his tour continues in a sketchbook now in the Glasgow School of Art.
10 June	Padua and Vicenza.
10–14 June	Verona.
14 June	Mantua.
14–15 June	Cremona.
15–16 June	Brescia.
17 June	Bergamo.
18 June	Lecco and Lake Como.
19–25 June	Cadenabbia.
26 June	Como.
27 June – 7 July	Milan. On 7 July Mackintosh left for Pavia and homewards.

APPENDIX III

Contents of sketchbooks

Recto pages of all three sketchbooks were numbered with odd numbers, most likely by Dr Henry Farmer. For the purpose of this listing, *verso* pages have been assigned the corresponding even numbers.

The Scottish sketchbook (2011 TX)

Cover: the original cover has been lost. Sheets measure 13.5cm x 18cm, or less.
Contents: 38 pp. Thirteen pages, scattered at intervals throughout the book, are blank. Four leaves have been removed, leaving page stubs.

Page

1   Three inscriptions:

      C=R=M

      Sketchbook (3) of / Charles Rennie Mackintosh

      From Oscar Paterson 1916 (within cartouche)

      (Sketch) Mosaic fragment, most likely after drawing by Anderson, W.J. (1890). *Architectural Studies in Italy*, plate IV.

2   Profiles and details of ornamental moulding.

3   Unidentified bell-tower and four slender towers or turrets (Figure 1).

4   Arch with Romanesque-like ornamentation: foliage and figurative.

5   Unused.

6   Details of Gothic roof construction. Cross-section, possibly of pier (Figure 2).

7   Loped trefoil and profile detail.

8–11   Unused.

–   One leaf removed between pages 8 and 9. This, and other removed pages, was cut before pagination, most likely by Mackintosh.

12   Mural tomb of Bailie Patrick Hunter, Churchyard of St Mary the Virgin, Crail, Fifeshire (Plate 1).

13   Mural tomb of Durie and Hamilton family, Crail.

14   Mural tomb of John Mackieson, Crail (Inscribed).

15   Unidentified building, possibly in Fifeshire (Plate 2).

16	Kirkgate, Linlithgow (Inscribed) (Plate 3).
17	Tomb, possibly part of the Livingstone family crypt, St Michael's Parish Church, Linlithgow (Inscribed).
18	Unused.
–	One leaf removed.
19	Carved panel, altar of St Mary of Pity, Glasgow Cathedral (Inscribed) (Plate 4).
20	Unidentified cottage.
21	Four architectural motifs, Culross, Fifeshire (Inscribed) (Plate 5).
22	Vegetation (Inscribed) (Plate 6).
–	One leaf removed.
23	Unused.
24	Apse, St Michael's, Linlithgow (Inscribed) (Plate 7).
25	Unused.
26	South elevation, St Michael's, Linlithgow (Inscribed) (Plate 8).
–	One leaf removed.
27	Apse, Church of the Holy Rude, Stirling (Inscribed).
28	Details of Stirling High School extension by J. MacLaren. Tower of Stirling's Tolbooth by Sir W. Bruce (Inscribed) (Plate 9).
29	West tower, Church of the Holy Rude, Stirling (Inscribed) (Plate 10).
30	Balustrade, Cowane's Hospital, Stirling (Plate 11).
31	Stirling Castle (Inscribed) (Plate 12).
32	Unused.
33	North elevation, Church of the Holy Rude, Stirling (Inscribed) (Figure 3).
34	Unused.
35	Details of south elevation, Church of the Holy Rude, Stirling (Inscribed) (Figure 4).
36	Unused.
37	Details of architectural ornament, Argyll's Lodgings, Stirling (Inscribed) (Plate 13).
38	Unused.

The Italian sketchbook (2009 TX)

Cover: original cloth cover, inscribed with Mackintosh's initials, measures 12.7cm x 17.7cm. Landscape format.

Contents: 93 pp. of pencil sketches, 12.6cm x 17.5cm, or smaller.

Inside cover inscriptions:

Chas. R. McIntosh / 140 Bath St. / Glasgow

[During 1893 Mackintosh changed the spelling of his name from McIntosh.]

Sketch book [sic] (1) of

[Inserted at some unknown date above, in a hand other than Mackintosh's, probably that of Henry George Farmer.]

(Label, below right): *G. Davidson, / Artists' Colourman, / 125 Sauchiehall St. / Glasgow.*

(Below left and transverse): Inscribed with what appears to be five Italian locations written in light pencil. These cannot with full certainty be deciphered.

Page

1   Inscribed:

    Oscar Paterson was an artist in stained glass. Specimens / of his work may be seen in Kirkwall Cathedral. He married / Sarah Kerrigan of Birr Barracks, Eire, & I taught / their eldest child – Oscar James – the violin. / Henry Farmer of Birr. / From Oscar Paterson. / Bath St. Glasgow

    ['Bath St. Glasgow', the address of Paterson's studio until c. 1930, was added later.]

2   Unused.

3   Details of gateposts and balustrades.

4   Unidentified church, possibly Scottish (Inscribed) (Plate 14).

5   Window and door details, perhaps Old College, Glasgow.

6   Unused.

7   Details, 1888 International Exhibition Hall by J. Sellars (Figure 5).

8   Details, possibly of same.

9   Details, possibly of same.

10   Unused.

11	1888 International Exhibition Hall by J. Sellars (Plate 15).
12	Pediment detail and unidentified monument/tomb (Inscribed).
13	Details, some of Kilnaughten Church, Co. Limerick, Ireland, copied from _Architect_, Vol. 18, 15 December 1877 (Inscribed) (Plate 16).
14	Amisfield Tower, Dumfries and Galloway (Inscribed) (Plate 17).
15	Aldie Castle, Perth and Kinross (Inscribed) (Plate 18).
16	Unidentified castle, most likely Scottish (Figure 9).
17	Details of battlements, most likely Scottish.
18	Two roughly sketched elevations, possibly Scottish.
19	Plan of barracks, unidentified.
20	Fountain, possibly copied from illustration of fountain at Cardiff Castle, designed by W. Burges, _Architect_, Vol. 18, 11 August 1877.
21	Details of window or niche, possibly Italian.
22	Tomb of David Kyle, Melrose Abbey churchyard (Inscribed) (Plate 19).
23	Two octagonal towers (Plate 20).
24	Details of Skelmorlie's Aisle, Largs, Ayrshire (Inscribed and dated) (Plate 21).
25	Monument of Sir Robert Montgomerie, Largs, Ayrshire (Inscribed).
26	Profile details of same (Inscribed and dated).
27	Brief detail, possibly door frame.
28	Door and details of neo-Greek jamb and lintel ornamentation (Inscribed).
29	Thomsonesque anthemion and palm-leaf ornament, measured (Figure 6).
30	Cairney Building, Bath Street, Glasgow by Alexander Thomson (Plate 22).
31	Seated nude figure, most likely statuary.
32	Brief architectural details.
33	Details of neo-Greek ornament (Inscribed).
34	Details of neo-Greek ornament.
35	Door and details of jamb moulding (Inscribed).
36	Architectural details: gables, tower and balustrades.
37	Architectural ornament, perhaps Thomson-designed wrought-ironwork.
38	Unidentified interior detail, possibly after design by Thomson.

The botanical sketchbook (2010 TX)

Cover: black leather and cloth with '*Sketchbook*' in gold lettering. Measures 17.7cm × 12.7cm.

Inside cover	Inscription: *From / Oscar Paterson / Bath Street / Glasgow* (within cartouche)
	Sketch book (2)
Recto frontispiece	Inscription: *Charles Rennie Mackintosh and / The Modern Movement (1952), 197. / 'Those lovely lace-like drawings / − Japanese in character − .../ reveal a highly developped [sic] faculty / for precise observation of detail / and a complete understanding of / structural form'.*
Verso frontispiece	Inscription: *Chas. R. Mackintosh / 140 Bath St / Glasgow.*
	Oxford 1895.

Page	
—	One leaf removed
1,2	Unused.
3	Orchid, probably a *Cymbidium*, and a single delphinium inflorescence (Plate 51).
4, 5	*Antirrhinum majus*, snapdragon (double page).
6	*Antirrhinum* (Plate 52).
7	*Helleborus niger*, Christmas rose (Inscribed. The thumb mark on the upper part of the page has been conserved as an integral part of the work) (Plate 53).
8	Blossom and leaf of gooseberry bush (Inscribed) (Plate 54).
9	Possibly *Saponaria*, rock soapwort (Inscribed) (Plate 55).
10	*Aconitum napellus*, monkshood (Inscribed).
11	*Aconitum napellus*, monkshood (Inscribed) (Plate 56).
12	*Iberis sempervirens*, candytuft and *Patati*, flower of the potato plant (Inscribed) (Plate 57).
13	Campanula medium, bells of Canterbury (Inscribed).
14, 15	*Althaea rosea*, hollyhock (double page, Inscribed) (Plate 58).
16, 17	Lily (double page, Inscribed) (Plate 59).
18	*Lunaria*, honesty (Inscribed) (Plate 60).
19	Unused.

SELECT BIBLIOGRAPHY

Billcliffe, Roger (1977). *Architectural Sketches and Flower Drawings by Charles Rennie Mackintosh.* London: Academy Editions.

Billcliffe, Roger (1995). *Mackintosh Watercolours.* London: John Murray.

Brett, David (2000). *C.R. Mackintosh: The Poetics of Workmanship (2nd edition).* London: Reaktion.

Burkhauser, Jude, editor (1990). *The Glasgow Girls.* Edinburgh: Canongate Press.

Chierici, Gino (1964). *Il Palazzo Italiano dal Secolo XI al Secolo XIX.* Milan: Antonio Vallardi Ed.

Crawford, Alan (1995). *Charles Rennie Mackintosh.* London: Thames and Hudson.

Finucci, Maria Christina (1986). *Il Viaggio in Italia di Charles Rennie Mackintosh. Critica D'Arte (gennaio/marzo),* pp. 55–64.

Howarth, Thomas (1977). *Charles Rennie Mackintosh and the Modern Movement (2nd edition).* London: Routledge & Kegan Paul (1st edition published 1952).

Kaplan, Wendy, editor (1996). *Charles Rennie Mackintosh.* New York, London and Paris: Abbeville Press.

Moffat, Alistair (1989). *Remembering Charles Rennie Mackintosh: An Illustrated Biography.* Lanark: Colin Baxter Photography Ltd.

Neat, Timothy (1994). *Part Seen, Part Imagined.* Edinburgh: Canongate Press.

Robertson, Pamela, editor (1990). *Charles Rennie Mackintosh: The Architectural Papers.* Wendlebury: White Cockade Publishing.

Robertson, Pamela (1995). *Charles Rennie Mackintosh: Art is the Flower.* London: Pavilion Books.

Robertson, Pamela, editor (1999). *Charles Rennie Mackintosh: Architectural Sketches.* Glasgow: Hunterian Art Gallery.